READING *BILLY BUDD*

# READING *BILLY BUDD*

*Hershel Parker*

NORTHWESTERN UNIVERSITY PRESS          EVANSTON, ILLINOIS

Published by Northwestern University Press
Evanston, Illinois 60201

Printed in the United States of America

ISBN #0-8101-0961-1 (cloth)
          0962-X (paper)

Library of Congress Cataloging in Publication Data

Parker, Hershel.
    Reading Billy Budd / Hershel Parker.
        p.      cm.
    Includes bibliographical references.
    ISBN 0-8101-0961-1 (cloth). — ISBN 0-8101-0962-X (paper)
    1. Melville, Herman, 1819–1891.  Billy Budd.  I. Title.
PS2384.B7P37    1990
813′.3—dc20                                          90-21487
                                                        CIP


The paper used in this publication meets the minimum requirements of American National
Standard for Information Sciences—Permanence of Paper for Printed Library Materials, ANSI
Z39.48-1984.

# Contents

*For*
*Harrison Hayford*
*and*
*Merton M. Sealts, Jr.*

# Acknowledgments

Mark Niemeyer generously helped me when I needed help, a week into the composition of this book. Donald Blume verified quotations in the first full printout, and Kevin J. Hayes helped with last-minute checking. Russell J. Reising read the manuscript carefully, and Alma MacDougall meticulously copy-edited the final version. Robert Jay Haber and Dr. Roslyn A. Haber gave timely and zestful encouragement. I revised many passages in response to wise criticisms first from Heddy-Ann Richter then from Professor Nathalia Wright. For any study of *Billy Budd, Sailor* the greatest thanks go to the two scholars to whom this book is dedicated, Harrison Hayford and Merton M. Sealts, Jr.

READING *BILLY BUDD*

# *Billy Budd* as Late Masterpiece

WHEN A GREAT WRITER LIVES TO AN ADVANCED AGE, PRODUCTIVE TO the last or productive *at* the last, we as readers take any final work as a legacy to be cherished far more than a book written in mid-career, but we like our late masterpieces better if they are short. Teachers of old-fashioned "major authors" survey courses are especially drawn to short final masterpieces because they are easy to assign in classes where writers as important as Walt Whitman and Emily Dickinson are each allotted, at most, three or four days. In such courses we can skip from some early Hemingway stories and *The Sun Also Rises* to *The Old Man and the Sea*, eliminating the treacherous terrain that stretches from before *The Green Hills of Africa* on *Across the River and Into the Trees*. We are especially happy when we can conclude that the last little work of a long career is a transcendent epitome of all the efforts of the artist's life, the triumph of an old age in which he or she still kept intellectual and aesthetic faculties intact and could tersely embody reflections on the grand themes that had preoccupied him or her during half a century or more of creativity. There is another twist: along with a tight tying up of old, mighty, and often harrowing themes, we want our examples of final grandeur to be reconciling if not downright soothing. We like *Oedipus Rex* even better because Sophocles lived to write *Oedipus at Colonus* as well, and when a writer as great as Shakespeare deprives us of an ideal late short suitably tamed tragedy we make the best we can of what we have— as when we read *The Tempest* as Shakespeare's unproblematical and blessedly short "long farewell" to his creative magic. Last short masterpieces are so important to us, no matter how sophisticated we are, that we approach them solemnly, like grown children gathering around the deathbed of a patriarch or matriarch, or, still more primitively, like tribespeople around the deathbed of a shaman. Hoping to catch the ultimate, hitherto-secret or hitherto-ungrasped word which links the human condition to the afterworld, we prefer above all to find short final masterpieces which are not just late-in-life but actually posthumous, since works published after an author's death (with obvious exceptions such as E. M. Forster's long pigeonholed *Maurice*) may embody not merely the author's message hissed or muttered in the face of death but an ultimate message from beyond the grave.

In 1916 readers were delighted with the news that Mark Twain had left at his death in 1910 a final unpublished book-length manuscript—*The Mysterious Stranger*, a work that in the 1950s (when American literature at last was taught in all colleges) turned out to be a wonderfully teachable epitome of Mark Twain's final pessimism. But a problem with the entire category of late, posthumous works is that they tend to be posthumous because they were not quite ready for print. Indeed, they may have been very far from being ready for print. Literary executors may want so strongly to capitalize on an author's fame that they may even fake a final work. Because Nathaniel Hawthorne had become immensely marketable after his death and had left few bank notes but many leaves of manuscript, his enterprising son Julian disingenuously patched together *Doctor Grimshaw's Secret* from surviving drafts; that work never achieved the status of a late masterpiece, but its fraudulent status went almost unchallenged for a century. In recent decades most teachers have stopped talking much about *The Mysterious Stranger* because in the 1960s scholars pointed out that Mark Twain's literary executor, Albert Bigelow Paine, had so strongly wanted Mark Twain to have written a late short masterpiece that he put parts of different drafts together, removing characters, combining characters, and giving the uneducated author a helping hand with the prose. There are never quite enough late final masterpieces to meet the demand, so the loss of one from the category causes another to be squeezed into its place. Now that *The Mysterious Stranger* is no longer seen as a teachable work, and now that shifting sexual attitudes and the vagaries in Hemingway's reputation prevent *The Old Man and the Sea* from common use in the classroom, about the nearest we come in survey courses to having an American equivalent of Sophocles' late short masterpiece is Herman Melville's *Billy Budd*. It was never completed; after Melville's death in 1891 it was kept for three decades in a tin bread-box in various locations in Manhattan, New Jersey, and Massachusetts (in constant peril from accidental fire or overzealous housecleaning, if not deliberate destruction with other batches of family papers); and in 1924 it was published at last in an imperfect text (flawed through editorial ineptitude, not chicanery), where, among other oddities, what was labeled the "Preface" was really only a discarded portion of a late chapter. Nevertheless, this text (entitled *Billy Budd, Foretopman*) was hailed at once as a masterpiece, and the story, in that text and subsequent texts, and read by different audiences, has kept that high status ever since.

*The Mysterious Stranger* seemed indubitably a testament of bleakness, before its status was cast into doubt, but *Billy Budd* was and is regularly taken as Melville's last will and spiritual or intellectual testament—with no consensus on what that testament says. This is not a one-book problem, for what we think of *Billy Budd* involves how we read and teach the trajectory of Melville's whole career. Some readers (mainly teachers in their role of critic) have argued passionately that *Billy Budd* constitutes Melville's "testament of acceptance" of the ways of God to mankind and others have argued (with equal fervor) that it constitutes his "testament of resistance" against all tyranny, whether in earthly societies or the cosmos. Students inevitably divide just as their elders have divided, and *Billy Budd* has proved to be problematical in the classroom, a strenuous and often frustrating test of the aesthetic and ideological presuppositions of teachers and students alike. Even though readers have not yet decided how to read the story, no one has challenged its immense significance. *Billy Budd* therefore occupies a prominent niche in the canon of American Literature— the secure-looking but always challenged and always shifting body of classic American texts—yet occupies it somewhat precariously, for its reputation has never been grounded on its anomalous status as an incomplete and imperfect work.

Although I talk about what critics of American literature write and what teachers and students do in literature courses, I am also writing for students and professors from other fields and for the now rare but always sought-for non-academic readers. To be sure, most of the copies of a book entitled *Reading "Billy Budd"* will be purchased by college libraries and those copies will be used most often by undergraduates (not necessarily English majors) or by graduate students in English departments, so I will now and at other times address these students directly. Since some undergraduates are skeptical when first told that they come to college (and even high school) equipped with a battery of aesthetic and ideological assumptions, the "problematical" *Billy Budd* can be a salutary provocative to a student who begins to take inventory of the assumptions in his or her footlocker or duffel bag. Indeed, a chief value of *Reading "Billy Budd"* is that it can help students (undergraduate or graduate) and general readers recognize that (like the idea or not) they already have a place in the history of American literary scholarship, criticism, and theory, and that they are free to think themselves into a place they are more at home in, if they want to. I review the history of *Billy Budd* in a way that can help readers think about how it and other novels came to be considered masterpieces, and I use the story's exceptional yet exemplary history as a way of helping readers understand the history of American literary scholarship, criticism, and theory. My aim has been to introduce the problematical qualities of *Billy Budd* to anyone who innocently loves literature and is willing to rethink, sophisticatedly, the notion that a classic piece of literature is always perfect, complete, and utterly interpretable, permanently ensconced in its lofty status after a process of screening which (however little anyone seems to remember about it) must have been judicious, wary, and exhaustive. For my part, examining the history and reputation of *Billy Budd* has left me more convinced than before that it deserves high stature (although not precisely the high stature it holds, whatever that stature is) and more convinced that it is a wonderfully teachable story—as long as it is not taught as a finished, complete, coherent, and totally interpretable work of art.

Anyone who has more than casual interest in *Billy Budd* must express gratitude to Harrison Hayford and Merton M. Sealts, Jr., for the years of work and thought embodied in their edition of

*Billy Budd, Sailor (An Inside Narrative)* (Chicago: University of Chicago Press, 1962), which contains both the now-standard "Reading Text" and the "Genetic Text" (showing the growth of the manuscript word and phrase by word and phrase). Resisting any urge to interpret the story themselves, they asked, at one point, a series of brilliant questions which they thought had to be answered before one could take a stand on the ultimate meaning and value of *Billy Budd*:

> [W]hat was the retired customs inspector, who had long ago written *Moby Dick*, accomplishing in the leisurely process of proliferating revision that occupied his "quiet, grass-growing" last years, a process terminated by the death of the author rather than the completion of his manuscript? In many of the late pieces, it would appear, he accomplished little—he was puttering. In *Billy Budd*, however, he achieved a work that has entered the canon of major American fiction and is usually listed second to *Moby Dick* among his novels. Wherein lay the difference between *Billy Budd* and the other late pieces? Did its quality of greatness emerge with one transforming major stroke somewhere in the gradual process of growth by accretion? Were all the instances of his minute verbal revision necessary to its greatness, or were many of them merely nervous or fussy gestures? To what extent do the revisions show a sure intuition of what was vital in the work as it stood at the end in semi-final manuscript? To what extent are many of the revisions purely random strokes that overlie and obscure the emerging conception? Into what categories do the stylistic revisions fall? Similar questions about the process of revision will occur to every reader. Many problems relevant to interpretation and evaluation will likewise suggest themselves— interrelated problems about form, theme, and language, to which study of the Genetic Text may suggest answers. (33-34)

Knowing that these questions could be answered by painstaking study of the evidence they offered of the composition of the manuscript, Hayford and Sealts hopefully couched part of their introductory material as "perspectives for criticism."

One might think that questions so fresh, provocative, and exciting would have set off a stampede among critics impatient for a challenge worthy of their skills. Nothing like that happened. Some teachers who had built their classroom performances and their crit-

ical essays around the centrality of the "preface" rued the loss of
something sanctified by their ritual use of it, going so far, at times,
as to say that the familiarity of the false "preface" made it part of
the text whether Melville intended it to be so or not. All critics—
from New Critics of the 1950s to the New Historicists of the late
1980s—continued to interpret the book as if it were a complete
and finally polished work of art; even the most aggressive Decon-
structionists of the early 1980s could not muster their tools for
dismantling it unless they were innocently confident that they were
starting their demolition with a perfect verbal icon. Saying so
sounds very strange, but this *Reading "Billy Budd"* is the first
study to try to answer any of Hayford and Sealts's questions. That
odd circumstance leads me to design this book not only as a guide
to Melville's last story but also as a guide to the Hayford-Sealts
edition, especially the "Genetic Text," the great treasure-house of
information about Melville's artistry which, after my initial plun-
dering, still lies open to exploration by anyone who wants to understand *Billy Budd*.

Hayford and Sealts's "Reading Text" is based upon their full
transcription of the manuscript, which is printed as the "Genetic
Text" in the second half of the 1962 hardback edition. The University of Chicago paperback Phoenix edition of *Billy Budd, Sailor*
contains the editors' "Growth of the Manuscript," "History of the
Text," and "Perspectives for Criticism"; then it contains their
"Reading Text," followed by "Notes & Commentary," "Bibliography," and "Textual Notes." The University of Chicago paperback
Midway Reprint series was designed to keep available important
books for which there is limited demand; in this series *"Billy
Budd": The Genetic Text* has appeared (but in fact has not been
kept in print). The Midway edition includes "Growth of the Man-
uscript" and "History of the Text," the "Analysis of the Manuscript," "Table & Discussion of Foliations," then "The Genetic
Text: Transcription," followed by "Stage *A* leaves," "Final Leaves,"
"Extra-Textual Leaves," and "Leaves with Inscribed Versos." The
reader who wants to check my page references to *Billy Budd, Sailor*
will need the University of Chicago hardback or else *both* the
Phoenix and Midway paperbacks. (The forthcoming Northwestern-
Newberry edition of *Billy Budd, Sailor* will include the Hayford-

Sealts "Genetic Text"; the wording of the text based on this "Genetic Text" will be all but identical to the Hayford-Sealts "Reading Text," though there will be many differences in such matters as punctuation and spelling, to conform with the policy of the Northwestern-Newberry Edition.)

# Unfinished MS: From Writing-Desk to Bread-Box

*Chapter One*

## Melville and the Historical Background of *Billy Budd*

MELVILLE DID NOT HAVE TO USE A SOURCEBOOK OR DO BASIC HISTORI-
cal research for *Billy Budd*: he could draw on his reserves of information that had never been set down in books. As a graybeard he
carried thick historical contexts in his own brooding consciousness,
much of it from what had been in his youth not so much a source
of preference as the source which was most often available—oral
history. Having lived at sea for weeks in 1839 then for many months
in the early 1840s, when yarn-spinning after labor was a cherished
art and a social obligation, Melville remembered many sailors
whose stories of bloody maritime struggles stretched back into the
eighteenth century, beyond the mutinies on British ships in 1797
at Spithead and the Nore which formed the immediate background
of his story. He probably was writing of himself in this passage
from *White-Jacket* (ch. 74): "I always endeavored to draw out the
oldest Tritons into narratives of the war-service they had seen.
There were but few of them, it is true, who had been in action;
but that only made their narratives the more valuable" (311). In
late 1849, during his trip to London to sell *White-Jacket*, Melville
chatted with an old American Negro who was a pensioner at the
sailors' hospital at Greenwich (where the body of Lord Nelson had
lain in state), probably the man he described in *Billy Budd* as a
Negro who had been with Nelson in 1805 when the British fleet
defeated the French and Spanish at Trafalgar. Melville knew many
older seamen who had fought in the War of 1812 and who had
heard with their own ears, from *their* elders, stories of personal

experiences going back far into the eighteenth century. (It helps to remember that Melville's parents made a wartime marriage, and that the War of 1812 was as close to Melville as the Vietnam War is to undergraduates of the 1990s.) Living as we do in an era when children and young people do not often listen to their elders reminisce hour by hour, day after day, it is hard to get into mind how many hours Melville may have spent hearing oral history—very likely more than the average college student of today has spent watching newsreel footage and Hollywood portrayals of wars and social upheavals of this century.

A good portion of Melville's fund of oral history came, of course, from landsmen, particularly from older relatives who had themselves taken part in the American Revolution or been intimate with patriots, or who had witnessed, on French soil, some of the immediate aftermath of the French Revolution. He heard many stories of the American Revolution from participants in those events (his paternal grandfather was after all coasting through old age in Boston on his exploits as an "Indian" at the Tea Party, and during Herman's summer visits would have regaled the lad with them). In the mid-1830s Melville heard stories of Paris in the time of Napoleon from his uncle who had lived there and moved in American and foreign diplomatic circles. (His own father had lived in France at that time, and spoke and wrote French.)

Melville was a reader of histories as well as a listener to oral history, and in his middle decades he spent far more time reading than conversing. During his early career Melville often borrowed or bought books, including histories, in order to plunder them for whatever book he was writing. During the mid-to-late 1880s he sometimes consulted libraries as a scholarly researcher trying to find answers to questions about historical conditions. Though at no time in his life was he the sort of precisionist who would make a plot turn on a point of law or historical accuracy, he aimed to make *Billy Budd* as accurate as he could on some technical details, and his researches were probably curtailed not by lack of curiosity but by lack of physical energy.

As a child and as a young man Melville had confronted the fact that while the American ideal was equal opportunity for all the bitter reality was that privilege was for the few. In the first years of his career, as he followed his late brother Gansevoort in burnishing the Melville name (though not reviving the family fortune), he came to share the ebullient mood of Manifest Destiny. Sharing this mood meant glossing over the militaristic embodiment of that mood in the war on Mexico, meant putting out of mind, from day to day, the reality of Negro slavery in the South, and ignoring as well as he could the legally enforced remanding of fugitive slaves from the North back to the South (something hard to do when his father-in-law, Lemuel Shaw, the Chief Justice of the Massachusetts Supreme Court, was one of the judicial remanders). The ideal of America as the Chosen Land and Americans as the Chosen People burst out most fervently in the two books Melville wrote in the summer of 1849, *Redburn* (1849) and *White-Jacket* (1850). In the first (ch. 58) he declared that if the Irish survivors of the potato famine can get to the United States, "they have God's right to come": "For the whole world is the patrimony of the whole world; there is no telling who does not own a stone in the Great Wall of China" (292). In *White-Jacket* (ch. 36) he proclaimed the United States as the new Israel:

> And we Americans are the peculiar, chosen people—the Israel of our time; we bear the ark of the liberties of the world. Seventy years ago we escaped from thrall; and, besides our first birthright—embracing one continent of earth—God has given to us, for a future inheritance, the broad domains of the political pagans, that shall yet come and lie down under the shade of our ark, without bloody hands being lifted. . . . Long enough have we been skeptics with regard to ourselves, and doubted whether, indeed, the political Messiah had come. But he has come in *us*, if we would but give utterance to his promptings. And let us always remember that with ourselves, almost for the first time in the history of earth, national selfishness is unbounded philanthropy; for we can not do a good to America but we give alms to the world. (151)

No American after Vietnam can read these words without a sense of irony; some contemporaries of Melville, Thoreau among them, who lived their daily lives acutely conscious of America's national sin of slavery, could not have read them when they were published without a bitter sense of irony. Other writings by Melville, even from the early years of his career, make it clear that such passages as these are isolated bursts of hopeful rhetoric from the height of his early ambition and the peak of his popularity. Long before the beginning of his two decades as an inspector at the New York Custom House, 1866-85, Melville suffered, as any idealist would have, a gradual disillusionment, and during the years following the centennial of the American declaration of independence he self-mockingly wrote into his "Burgundy Club" pieces a demagogic Colonel J. Bunkum who celebrates Americans as a people "to whose custody Jehovah has entrusted the sacred ark of human freedom."

Current themes were inescapable to anyone in the New York Custom House, where bribery was a way of life and every employee (it is asserted) was forced to contribute to Republican campaigns or be fired. In his 1951 biography (Berkeley: University of California Press; reprinted 1981) Leon Howard suggests (329) that when Melville wrote the series of "Burgundy Club" sketches (apparently between 1875 and 1877) "the mistakes of Reconstruction, the political problems of President Grant, and his own resentment of the new Grand Army of the Republic were still fairly fresh" in his mind. On 7 March 1877 (the week Hayes became president) Melville could profess himself indifferent to the Republican theft of the national election of 1876 from the Democrats (though in truth his indifference was not new—he may never have voted in his life). Yet he could rail, at times, on the conventionality of the world as a man who had survived into a period when individuality had been homogenized, when values had been lost, when national ideals had been polluted, when local, state, and federal governments had become equal in corruption rather than in integrity, when organized religion and conventional morality had gained power over public thought, and when only an old skeptic like himself (once slurred in the press as an atheist) was devoting serious thought to the possible validity of the doctrine of original sin—a concept which (as far as most people were concerned) had been replaced by what we would call psycho-babble. But even when commenting on recent political events Melville tended to see them as manifestations of old issues of his youth and early manhood.

Leon Howard pointed out that by the early 1880s Melville's mind "had already become more at home in the past" (330). Melville's impulse to reminisce, and to contrast his humble occupation of deputy customs inspector with his family's status in pre-

vious generations, had been evident for years. In the late 1860s or
early 1870 Melville, in preparing an account of his uncle Thomas
Melvill's career for a *History of Pittsfield*, found himself working
with evocative materials, his uncle's stories of Paris during the
Napoleonic era. The new French Revolution in 1871 reminded him
of what he had heard and read of the "first French Revolution" (as
he called the 1789 revolution in his note to "The Conflict of
Convictions" in *Battle-Pieces* [1866]), as well as his own memories
of the tumult throughout much of Europe in 1848, the year before
he saw Paris. National centennials celebrated in 1875 and 1876
then in 1887 also reminded him of old political themes, as did his
own family's active interest in history and genealogy. Clearly, also,
Melville kept well informed about other European revolutionary
movements of the 1860s and 1870s. He was well into *Billy Budd*
by 1889, when a barrage of publicity in the newspapers and magazines marked the centennial of the French Revolution.

Among these old political themes which Melville explored in
*Clarel* (1876) and the "Burgundy Club" sketches were some commonplaces from his youth: the idea of the American West as a
safety valve that would prevent the East from exploding into a class
war; the dubious possibility that America was the New Paradise
and that the Americans were the Chosen People; the concern that
"leveling" would take the savor from American life; the tendency
to posit democratic "ultraism" as the foe of inherited, aristocratic
traditions; the idea that America was dangerously cutting itself off
from the lessons of the past; and the idea that the French Revolution had been essentially different from the American Revolution.
In the 1870s when Melville brooded on the old theme of the
leveling tendencies in American life, it was not political leveling so
much as spiritual leveling that aroused his anxiety. In *Clarel* (bk.
1, canto 34), as a group of pilgrims look thoughtfully over Jerusa-
lem, Rolfe (often the proponent of Melville's views) says:

> "All now's revised:
> Zion, like Rome, is Niebuhrized.
> Yes, doubt attends. Doubt's heavy hand
> Is set against us; and his brand
> Still warreth for his natural lord—
> King Common-Place—whose rule abhorred
> Yearly extends in vulgar sway,

> Absorbs Atlantis and Cathay;
> Ay, reaches toward Diana's moon,
> Affirming it a clinkered blot,
> Deriding pale Endymion.
> Since thus he aims to level all,
> The Milky Way he'll yet allot
> For Appian to his Capital."
>
> (lines 18-31)

Here Melville echoes the plaints that Romantic poets had lodged against the disillusioning effects of science, but in blaming the German historian Barthold Niebuhr for reducing myth to trivial fact Melville condemns historical skepticism and rationalism rather than science for tarnishing the myths that once had sustained belief and hope. When the character Vine muses that the Ishmaelites show "a lingering trace / Of some quite unrecorded race / Such as the Book of Job implies," he adds:

> "But, as men stray
> Further from Ararat away
> Pity it were did they recede
> In carriage, manners, and the rest;
> But no, for ours the palm indeed
> In bland amenities far West!"
>
> (2.27.74-76, 89-94)

Throughout the "Burgundy Club" sketches, as well as *Clarel*, Melville played with the conflict between aristocratic tradition and democratic egalitarianism, usually mocking both those who affect aristocratic "gew-gaws" and those levelers who would destroy anything hinting of inherited privileges, such as the badge of the Order of the Cincinnati awarded to a select group of Revolutionary officers. (Melville's grandfather Gansevoort's badge of the Cincinnati was a cherished heirloom, owned through much of Melville's life by his cousin Guert Gansevoort; Melville himself made do with his badge as deputy inspector for the Custom House.)

Of all the old political themes which Melville brooded upon in the 1870s, the French Revolution (as the archetypal modern revolution) seems most to have engrossed his thought. All his life the war which counted most was the French Revolution, and always the first French Revolution. The uprisings of 1848 and 1871 were merely manifestations of the old uncompleted eruption. One of the major characters of *Clarel*, Mortmain, in 1848 had been a professional revolutionary, full of "warm desires and schemes for man" (2.4.30). Rolfe sketches his story:

> Europe was in a decade dim:
> Upon the future's trembling rim
> The comet hovered. His a league
> Of frank debate and close intrigue:
> Plot, proselyte, appeal, denounce—
> Conspirator, pamphleteer, at once,
> And prophet. Wear and tear and jar
> He met with coffee and cigar:
> These kept awake the man and mood
> And dream. That uncreated Good
> He sought, whose absence is the cause
> Of creeds and Atheists, mobs and laws.
> Precocities of heart outran
> The immaturities of brain.
>
> (2.4.40-53)

Mortmain's present disillusionment is shared by all the serious-minded major characters. Yet the reforming instinct was one Melville could share, and he clearly knew that the English Romantic poets had at first been as "precocious" of heart as Mortmain. In a passage canceled from *Billy Budd*, he noted that the "opening proposition made by the Spirit of that Age" (the era of the French Revolution) "was one hailed by the noblest men of it. Even the dry tinder of a Wordsworth took fire" (377).

As Harrison Hayford and Merton M. Sealts, Jr., say, "the opposing positions" of Edmund Burke, author of *Reflections on the Revolution in France* (1790), and Thomas Paine, author of the rejoinder, *The Rights of Man* (1791), "concerning the doctrine of abstract natural rights lie behind the dialectic of *Billy Budd*" (138). Older men on both sides of his family had contributed to Melville's Burkean sense that the Anglo-American system in which freedom slowly broadens down from precedent to precedent is always surer than the French way of redressing wrong—anarchical and atheistic revolution. Yet Melville could not disown the inspiriting doctrines of Thomas Paine (like his character Mortmain a conspirator, pamphleteer, and prophet), and pointedly built the title *The Rights of Man* into his text. In his final form of chapter 7, Melville wrote of Captain Vere:

> His settled convictions were as a dike against those invading waters of novel opinion social, political, and otherwise, which carried away as in a torrent no few minds in those days, minds by nature not inferior to his own. While other members of that aristocracy to which by birth he belonged were incensed at the innovators mainly because their theories were inimical to the privileged classes, Captain Vere disinterestedly opposed them not alone because they seemed to him insusceptible of embodiment in lasting institutions, but at war with the peace of the world and the true welfare of mankind. (62-63)

Melville's distrust of the French Revolution was ambivalently qualified. The mutinying English sailors at the Nore, Melville said, ran up the British colors with the union and cross wiped out, "by that cancellation transmuting the flag of founded law and freedom defined, into the enemy's red meteor of unbridled and unbounded revolt" (54). He added, "Reasonable discontent growing out of practical grievances in the fleet had been ignited into irrational combustion as by live cinders blown across the Channel from France in flames" (54). One earlier draft referred frankly to "the enemy's red rag of revolt and universal revolution" (300), and in the canceled pages which until the Hayford-Sealts edition were mistaken as a preface, Melville was careful not to assert that the French Revolution had turned out to be a political advance along nearly the whole line for man—he changed "man" to read "Europeans" and made the sentence read that to "some" thinkers it had turned out so (378). Melville was unwilling to grant to the Revolution credit for ultimate benefits to Europeans, much less to all mankind. But on the next leaf he fell into saying that the Nore Mutiny though naturally deemed by Englishmen "monstrous at the time, doubtless gave the first latent prompting to those progressive reforms in the British navy which for its sailors makes it a service" to be faithful to (378). Some basis for his horror at the French Revolution is indicated in a draft of chapter 8 in which he wrote that some Americans dreaded that the era's "eclipsing menace mysterious and prodigious" (320) might spread across the Atlantic: "So I had it from venerable men know[n] to me in my youth" (321)—plainly a reference to men such as his grandfather Melvill.

Melville had described himself in a journal entry late in 1849 as "a pondering man," and he had become a remarkable one. As early as the late 1850s he was called a "cloistered thinker" (see Jay Leyda, *The Melville Log* [New York: Harcourt, Brace, 1951], 2: 606), and as the years passed he "'railed'" to his wife within his walls about matters of the country in general (as reported by his granddaughter Eleanor Melville Metcalf in *Herman Melville: Cycle and Epicycle* [Cambridge: Harvard University Press, 1953], 216). Also, "when the spirit moved him" (letter in the Houghton Library of Harvard University from Melville's daughter Frances Thomas to her daughter Eleanor Metcalf, 30 April 1925) he burst forth to his visitors "in full tide of talk—or rather of monologue" (*Log* 2: 605) and expounded "highly individual views of society and politics" (*Log* 1: 479). One of the younger men who talked with the slightly mellower Melville of the 1880s (and who perhaps caught him on a particularly genial day) remembered that "though a man of moods, he had a peculiarly winning and interesting personality," and recalled especially his habit of showing "gentle deference to an opponent's conventional opinion while he expressed the wildest and most emancipated ideas of his own" (*Library of the World's Best Literature Ancient and Modern*, ed. Charles Dudley Warner, 17: 9868). In the last decade of his life, he for the most part settled into a regard of the current politicians as "Damn fools!" (an often-repeated phrase his son-in-law still recalled in the late 1920s) and of himself as an "old fogy," as he put it in a letter of December 1880. The irony was that the political ideas which younger men could sometimes see as emancipated were for the most part outgrowths of commonplaces of Federalist thought; Melville, far from being a highly original political thinker (as some later critics have innocently said), was a "pondering man" who had brooded long upon the political themes of his youth and who had come to see even the issues of the Gilded Age in the Federalistic terms which he had absorbed in his youth. His political attitudes became more pronouncedly unusual merely by virtue of his longevity, since many of them were indeed formed under the "alleged bigoted Federalism of old times" (*Pierre*, bk. 15, sect. 1, 218). In the years after his retirement from the Custom House,

Melville was not meditating on current partisan political issues, which had seldom concerned him for long, but on the debates of his childhood and adolescence, when it was still very much an open question which was preferable, a monarchy or a republic, and where all the men of his family, Melvills or Gansevoorts, looked back with horror at the anarchy of the French Revolution. As he wrote his way into what became *Billy Budd, Sailor*, he was moving onto a familiar, and perhaps even comfortable philosophical terrain where the radical Thomas Paine and the conservative Edmund Burke were engaged in endless battle dubious of outcome, and where despite deep ambivalence his own allegiance was on the side of tradition, order, and incremental progress.

# Chapter Two

## *Billy Budd* in Melville's Late Literary Milieu

IN THE MID-1880S LEGACIES FROM RELATIVES FREED THE MELVILLES FROM financial strain for the first time in their married life so that they were not only long out of debt (the curse of the 1850s) and decently prosperous (as they had been since the early 1880s) but affluent—indeed, in the half decade before his death, they were by almost any standards rich, although the only change in their pattern of living was that his wife began to put twenty-five dollars into Melville's pocket every month with the unspoken understanding that it was his to spend freely on books and prints. Aside from that subtle but momentous change, the Melvilles did not spend their money differently, but they knew it was there. One practical consequence was that for the first time in his life Melville was not dependent upon the good will of publisher, reader, or reviewer but was free to pursue his literary projects as fully as he could do, allowing for the decline in his health, and free to pay a press to print what he wanted in the quantity he wanted for his private distribution among a dwindling circle of relatives—and an enlarging circle of admirers.

A change had occurred in Melville's literary status in the mid-1880s. A new generation of American newspaper and magazine editors gradually became aware that readers might be intrigued by a brief human-interest item (however inexact) on a once-famous author who was (to the astonishment of the public or at least the astonishment of the writer of the squib) still alive, a survivor of his fame. Such notoriety was not particularly pleasant to Melville, who asked rhetorically what he could do—retaliate? Even while these more or less inaccurate little items in American newspapers continued to inform readers that Melville was still alive, and had been buried alive all these years in the New York Custom House, a wholly different sort of mention began appearing in British magazines and began to be reprinted in the United States—extravagant praise for Melville's greatness combined with extravagant indignation that he was so little known at home. These tributes were delayed evidence of the very gradual and almost silent growth of Melville's reputation in England during the previous two decades, first among a handful, then among a few dozen or a few hundred youngish more-or-less radical literary people. Some of the most brilliant radical young literary men (from overlapping groups—pre-Raphaelites, or adherents of the workingmen's movement, or Fabian Socialists, or nautical writers) came to link Melville first with Whitman then also with Thoreau as great American writers neglected or even abused at home and still almost unknown to the British public and the British literary establishment. (See the "Historical Note" to the Northwestern-Newberry edition of *Moby-Dick*, 1988.) In 1883 the emerging British enthusiasm hit the American press, with a suggestion from the sea-writer W. Clark Russell that someone write a biography of Melville, so as to "let the world know as much as can be gathered of his seafaring experiences and personal story of the greatest genius your country has produced—leagues ahead of Longfellow and Bryant as a poet" (*Log* 2: 784). In 1884 Melville received the first (or the first to be preserved) of what became a trickle of letters from English admirers, and by 1885 tributes from those admirers were being reprinted in the United States and sometimes written especially for American papers. Amazingly, young admirers began pressing upon Melville books and articles that they or their friends had written about him or about other writers; they sought his opinion, hoping, of course, that his enthusiasm would match theirs. Out of courtesy and a genuinely shared interest, he read what they sent. Perhaps the high point of personal satisfaction for Melville in all this attention was his correspondence with Russell, which culminated in Melville's dedicating *John Marr and Other Sailors* to Russell in 1889 and in turn being the dedicatee of Russell's *An Ocean Tragedy* in 1889.

Several of these British admirers had learned of Melville from the Victorian poet James ("B.V.") Thomson, who was the first person to compare Melville and Whitman in print (as far as we know) and who spread Melville's fame among several of his own admirers in Leicester and London. After Thomson's early death some of his admirers corresponded with Melville and sent gifts of Thomson's works, among them the long poem "The City of Dreadful Night," now seldom read, which had a vogue among radical young British literary people. Early in 1886 Melville also received from James Billson, a young English admirer of Thomson, a "semi-manuscript" edition of Edward FitzGerald's free translation of the *Rubaiyat*. (At a time when correct copies were not available in England, Thomson had copied out the whole poem [as printed in 1859?], and Billson recalled in the 1920s that he had lent a transcription of the late Thomson's manuscript "to the Book editor at the Secular Hall" in Leicester, "who made a large number of copies which he sold at a trifling cost." One of these Billson sent Melville.) The gift of the *Rubaiyat* merely confirmed Melville's previous interest in FitzGerald's version of the quatrains of Omar Khayyam, whom Melville called "that sublime old infidel" in an April 1886 letter to Billson, probably on the basis of the 1878 Boston edition; he also bought soon after its publication the more elaborate Boston edition of 1886, illustrated by Elihu Vedder. In a letter to H. S. Salt on 12 January 1890 Melville described Thomson's "The City of Dreadful Night" as "the modern Book of Job, under an original poem duskily looming with the same aboriginal verities." But more strongly than Thomson's poem, FitzGerald's translation defined the era's emerging world-weariness and skepticism, and Melville's own disillusionment was undoubtedly soothed in his last years by the *Rubaiyat*. Contact with his British admirers drew Melville into participating in some aspects of the current or recent British literary scene, with the result that the tone of "old fogy" he had invested some energy in perfecting now became, at times, blurred with a world-weary tone owing more than a little to such writers as Thomson and FitzGerald. He cherished the Vedder edition, poring over the words and the illustrations for long sessions during the years he was working on *Billy Budd*. We know that he went so far as to identify with Vedder, for his widow later wrote to the painter: "He was 'proud to call you his countryman' he would say after an absorbed study of your work" (David Jaffe, "'Sympathy with the Artist': Elizabeth Melville and Elihu Vedder," *Melville*

*Society Extracts* 81 [May 1990]: 10). As a result of gifts and letters
from England Melville was drawn into a late-Victorian literary mi-
lieu more strongly than he might have been if he had gone his own
solitary way, reading magazines that came to hand and haunting
bookstores like a timid old wraith (as he was described), and reading only the books that he happened to encounter on his own.

One of the first writers about *Billy Budd*, John Freeman, called
that book Melville's everlasting yea, in reference to Thomas Carlyle's *Sartor Resartus* (1833-34). That is anachronistic. In his young
manhood Melville had been fascinated with Carlyle, who seemed
to him to be asking some of the biggest questions a thinker could
ask—about the relationship of Nature to God; about the possibility of being heroic in a Mammon-worshiping age when Democracy
was hurtling blindly on in alliance with Atheism; about the loss of
social order in an age in which privileges were being lost by the
worthy and gained by the unworthy (and when values were being
leveled down). Melville, like most idealistic young writers in the
English language—like Thoreau and Whitman in this country—
had gone through a Carlylean phase in his own development. Yet
the man who lived four weeks in a tropical Eden in his young
manhood then toiled nineteen of his middle and late years in the
New York Custom House was never given to fervent everlasting
yeas, and not apt, except under extreme excitement, to utter even
temporary or contingent yeas. The meditative narrative tone of
*Billy Budd* owes more to books that Melville read late in life, such
as the *Rubaiyat*, than to *Sartor Resartus*.

In its aesthetic aims *Billy Budd* may also be indebted to British
poets and critics Melville had been reading for a quarter of a
century or more. During the late 1850s and early 1860s, after his
literary career was over, Melville's reading of British poetry had
been little short of obsessive. Having in his young manhood written some of the greatest prose in the language without the dubious
advantage of a formal education, he then (in the autodidacticism
which was part of the genuine American spirit of the century), put
himself to school to the great and lesser poets of his native language, though seldom of his native country. At the same time he
conscientiously studied critics and historians who dealt with issues
of aesthetics either in verbal or visual arts. In his books from the
late 1850s onward he made notes on basic issues in aesthetics the

way he had, at thirty, made notes on basic theological and philosophical concepts. Reading such writers helped him clarify for himself his own then-obscure place in literary history and helped assuage him for the strange fate of his own ambition. That ambition between 1848 and the beginning of 1852 had been boundless— almost grotesquely high, had not some of what he was writing proved to be (as he dared to think) not unworthy of mention in the same breath with Shakespeare's plays. He was to be the writer of "a mighty book" (*Moby-Dick* 456) and more than one mighty book: *Moby-Dick* (1851) was a whale, but he had heard of greater creatures of the sea, and *Pierre* was to be such a "Kraken" book (letter to Hawthorne, 17? November 1851). But with the publication of *Pierre* (1852) he had suffered as bitter a lesson as any American has had on the vanity of human endeavors. By the time of his work on *Billy Budd* the agony of gigantic ambition was long passed beyond, lost in the aftermath of *Clarel* (what he had left after the fiasco of *Pierre*), but he continued privately to think about what constitutes literary greatness, and he did so in large part under the guidance of the British poets and critics.

Strong evidence of the impact of contemporary British poetry on the aesthetic ideas in *Billy Budd* is in the first volume of Melville's copy of Vasari's *Lives of the Most Eminent Painters, Sculptors, and Architects* (which he had with him in the years he wrote *Billy Budd*). There he made notes on how an artist achieves greatness:

> Attain the highest result.—
>     A quality of Grasp.—
> The habitual choice of noble subjects.—
>     The Expression.—
> Get in as much as you can.—
> Finish is completeness, fulness,
>     not polish.—

In working on *Billy Budd* Melville was no longer impelled to reach for what he could not quite grasp, but he was defining himself, old and humbled as he was, *against* the painter Andrea del Sarto as portrayed by Robert Browning. In Browning's poem "Andrea del Sarto," the main source of which was, as Melville appreciated, Vasari's *Lives*, the subtitle ("Called 'The Faultless Painter'") sets up the contrast between high professional competence and the higher grandeur attainable by great but less tidy genius. Like many of his contemporaries, Melville was struck by the poem's most challenging lines (already passing into proverbial status), Andrea's honest admission that the perfection of his own work dooms it to less than greatness: "Ah, but a man's reach should exceed his grasp, / Or what's a heaven for?" As he wrote *Billy Budd* Melville was at a stage of life when his reach did not, anymore, much exceed his grasp, and when he did not necessarily want it to, but he now could posit the opinions of aestheticians as well as his own instincts against his century's overvaluation of superficial perfection in art.

"Polish" had eluded Melville in his first years as a writer. In *Moby-Dick* (ch. 82) he had declared that in some enterprises a careful disorderliness is the true method. In the same book he recalled an overwhelming visual experience from his visit to the Rhine country in 1849—the crane on the uncompleted medieval tower of the cathedral of Cologne, a symbol for him of the fact that the most ambitious undertakings remain unfinished. By the time he became capable of "polish" he did not value it any more than Browning did in "Andrea del Sarto." In his last years, he expressed in *Billy Budd* a very similar suspicion of the literary work which is elaborated down to the last ornament, the structural and stylistic equivalent of a finial on a piece of furniture. (He knew that in Browning's poem the lines already quoted were followed by "all is silver-grey / Placid and perfect with my art: the worse!") A certain raggedness was more desirable than superficial perfection, more apt to accord with human nature and the rest of the world. This attitude should be recognized as one Melville had held to for many years, not a self-justification of a man so old and weak that he could not control his material. Some of the insoluble problems in the text of *Billy Budd* as he left it are due to an altogether natural decline in his "quality of Grasp" (or *duration* of grasp, or *comprehensiveness* of grasp), but Melville would not have wanted *Billy Budd* to be either placid or perfect.

## Chapter Three

---

## *Billy Budd* in Melville's Working Life

---

WHILE NOTHING LIKE A MONTH-BY-MONTH SCHEDULE OF MELVILLE'S work on *Billy Budd* can be established, some of the major phases can be dated in relation to events in his life and to his progress on his other literary efforts. At the time of his retirement on the last day of 1885 Melville was hardly strong enough to plan on writing a long book. His wife gave this description in January 1886 of how his work at the Custom House had worn him down: "For a year or so past he has found the duties too onerous for a man of his years, and at times of exhaustion, both mental and physical, he has been on the point of giving it up, but recovering a little, has held on, very naturally anxious to do so, for many reasons." She added: "He has a great deal [of] unfinished work at his desk which will give him occupation, which together with his love of books will prevent time from hanging heavy on his hands—and I hope he will get into a more quiet frame of mind, exempt from the daily irritation of over work." (The "unfinished work" may have included a ballad about a sailor named Billy Budd the night before his execution, and perhaps some related prose begun as a headnote to the ballad, one of several prefatory prose comments in which Melville expatiated on topics in the poems or on matters of interest to him, even if tangential to the poems as he had written them.) Healthfully distracting occupation was what Mrs. Melville had in mind, not another obsessive drive to create a literary masterpiece, and to all appearances what Melville did with the poem and headnote about Billy Budd was at about the level of concentration which pleased both of them.

Scholars, primarily Hayford and Sealts, have identified some of the "unfinished work" Mrs. Melville referred to, often relying on evidence such as the writing which survives only because Melville frugally turned over the pages and reused them in the *Billy Budd* manuscript. The projects consisted of many poems (some with associated prose passages) in varying states of completion, some dating back to the late 1850s, when Melville first hoped to publish a volume of poetry. Perhaps some of the poems of the late 1850s were incorporated into the "Parthenope" poems he worked on in the mid-1870s (known today as the "Burgundy Club" pieces, consisting of mixed prose and poetry). *Clarel* (finished at least a year or two before its publication in 1876) had allowed Melville the chance for private retrospective analysis of his relationship with Hawthorne, but most of the issues of the poem were public—the new intellectual, religious, and political issues of the era after the Civil War, seen in long historical perspective. With the enormous effort of *Clarel* behind him, the informal "Burgundy Club" sketches must have served Melville as self-consolation when he turned more inward, content to hold genial converse with his invented characters who, like him, were concerned with the fate of the values and the issues of his youth in the alien age of Reconstruction. In solitude he had his boon companions.

Soon after his retirement Melville took out the old "Burgundy Club" material again, and by around 1890 was thinking of publishing the poetic parts, now entitled "At the Hostelry" and "Naples in the Time of Bomba," without the prose sketches. Perhaps it was at this late stage that Melville wrote in pencil a prose preface called "House of the Tragic Poet" to precede another preface. As Robert A. Sandberg has shown, the speaker in "House of the Tragic Poet," a character Melville invented late in his work on the Burgundy Club material, is a gentleman of mature years who takes on the task of editing the material for publication ("'The Adjustment of Screens': Putative Narrators, Authors, and Editors in Melville's Unfinished *Burgundy Club* Book," *Texas Studies in Literature and Language* 31 [Fall 1989]: 426-50; see also Sandberg's "'House of the Tragic Poet': Melville's Draft of a Preface to His Unfinished Burgundy Club Book," *Melville Society Extracts* 79 [November 1989]: 1, 4-7). This editor (who has never before ventured into print) here argues that the famous "House of the Tragic

Poet" excavated at Pompeii is misnamed: anything as lavish as that Roman house and at the same time as inhospitable (there was a "Beware of the Dog" mosaic) must have belonged to a publisher, not a poet, and the canine mosaic must have been there to frighten away would-be authors. Melville portrays the editor as dreading the attempt to publish the sketches. Consulting an old friend who had "risen to an influential position as a member of the metropolitan press," and knows "all about Popular Opinion and the popular taste," the editor is given a number of reasons a publisher should decline the manuscript. The quotation which follows is from Sandberg's account ("'Adjustment of Screens'" 442-43):

> He [the friend] gave a catalog of reasons: the manuscript was not in "the current"; nothing new is told; the theme does not relate to America; the meter is "as old as the hills"; the events described in the "main piece" took place twenty years ago, "an aeon to the popular mind"; his [the editor's] method is "painterly," not photographic; and finally, worst of all—"I fail to see that anywhere you have laid an anchor to windward by conciliating the suffrages of the ladies, and in marked preference to those of the men." The tyro editor responds only to the last criticism: "The ladies?" The critic explains: "The ladies . . . arbiters of the social success of men, this have they become in the literary sphere, as to every book, the design of which is at all to please."

Revolving the possible ways of getting the best hearing for his book, the editor chances upon an old volume of miscellanies at a Nassau Street bookstall, and there finds good advice: "In reading a book skip not the preface: before publishing a book, if preface you have, drop it" (443). Very likely, Melville wrote this section during the period when he was, once again, venturing into print, editing his poems for publication and intermittently pushing along his manuscript about Billy Budd. Somewhere in his mind must have been memories of his humiliating failure to have his poems published in 1860, the even more humiliating failure of *Clarel* in 1876 (and his having to authorize the destruction of Putnam's remaining copies three years later), but Melville had achieved a wry, sardonic attitude toward the current literary scene, where (as William Dean Howells was proclaiming) the most successful writers were directing their words toward the chaste eyes of young American girls.

By late 1887 (if not well before that) Melville was working on a short prose and poetic manuscript, variously entitled, in which Rammon, a son of Solomon (an invented figure, not in the Bible) finds his father's Hebraic philosophy (in which there is no afterlife) challenged by the Buddhistic theme of immortality and transmigration of souls. (In 1888 Melville cannibalized the "Rammon" material for a lyric "The Enviable Isles" which he put into *John Marr* as "from 'Rammon.'") Melville sorted through and retouched other poetic and prose pieces, especially the works in the two volumes he lived to publish, *John Marr and Other Sailors, with Some Sea-Pieces* (1888) and *Timoleon and Other Ventures in Minor Verse* (1891). Early in 1890 he was absorbed in arranging a volume of verse for publication under the title *As They Fell*, to consist of two parts, "A Rose or Two" and "Weeds & Wildings," each with thirteen poems. *Billy Budd* needs to be seen in relation to many other pieces of "unfinished" literary work (some gradually brought to completion) and perhaps in relation to a certain number of new undertakings—not as the single obsessive labor of Melville's last lustrum.

In some of the poems drafted or reworked between the mid-1870s and his retirement, Melville moved far inward, not only away from the public poem *Clarel* but also more inward than in the "Burgundy Club" manuscripts where he savored the imagined conversations with worthy friends. Some of the late prose and poetry dealt with solitary old men or old men engaged in monologue to an audience of one. The little prose piece "Daniel Orme" reads much like the prose headnote to the poem "John Marr," and may possibly be a headnote that survived its poem. The prose descriptions of these two old sailors, Orme and Marr, have strong affinities with both the narrator in *Billy Budd* and one of the striking minor characters in that story, the old Dansker. ("Daniel Orme" was first published by Raymond Weaver in 1924, mistakenly labeled as "Omitted from 'Billy Budd.'") Whether Melville had drafted the poem "Billy in the Darbies" before or after he retired, the prose headnote to it began (Harrison Hayford and Merton M. Sealts, Jr., have shown) not as a new late literary departure, a deliberate return to longish fiction, but merely as a poem for the *John Marr* collection, one which, like "John Marr," acquired a headnote that eventually overshadowed the poem. In "Innocence and Infamy: *Billy*

Budd, Sailor" (in *A Companion to Melville Studies*, ed. John Bryant [Westport, Conn.: Greenwood Press, 1986], 407-30), Sealts makes this terse summation: "Melville began *Billy Budd, Sailor*, in the course of his work on the *John Marr* volume, for which the ballad entitled 'Billy in the Darbies' that now concludes the story was originally intended" (410).

In this 1986 essay Sealts emphasizes just how closely related *Billy Budd, Sailor* is to *John Marr and Other Sailors*. Not only was the poem "Billy in the Darbies" intended to go in the volume, Marr himself is in some ways very like the portrait of Melville as he presents himself in the narration of *Billy Budd, Sailor*. Sealts quotes from the "John Marr" headnote some of Marr's musings about his shipmates of long ago as "phantoms of the dead":

> As the growing sense of his environment threw him more and more upon retrospective musings, these phantoms . . . became spiritual companions, losing something of their first indistinctness and putting on at last a dim semblance of mute life; and they were lit by that aureola circling over any object of the affections in the past for reunion with which an imaginative heart passionately yearns. (411)

Marr's memories of merchant-sailors, huntsman-whalers, and man-of-war's men are given, Sealts points out, in the order of Melville's own nautical experiences, and other poems in *John Marr* "make more explicit references to associates of Melville's own past" (411). Sealts emphasizes the similarity of the narrative voice in the now-famous *Billy Budd, Sailor* to the voice in several other prose headnotes to poems:

> The narrator of *Billy Budd*, it may be observed, sounds very much like the authors of these several earlier headnotes—which is to say, like Melville himself. Twice he recalls specific incidents of Melville's own visits to England: at Liverpool in 1839 (p. 43: "now more than half a century ago") and at Greenwich in 1849 (p. 66: "now more than forty years ago"); he also alludes habitually to figures of history and literature that had long engaged Melville as well. (412)

As he aged, Melville's mind became thronged with faces of seamen he had known four decades and more earlier. He had never wholly banished them from his consciousness. In the first years of his literary career some of his shipmates had corresponded with him. In 1853 or afterwards Melville wrote down a full list of "*What became of the ship's company of the whale-ship 'Acushnet,' according to Hubbard who came home in her (more than a four years' voyage) and who visited me at Pittsfield.*" After his retirement, free to live if he pleased in memories of the distant past, Melville brooded over "what became of" his shipmates in whalers and in the U.S. Navy. *Billy Budd* gradually became an "inside narrative" which told all that had previously been put on human record about Billy and also told more than had ever been put on record. As he made it such a full, inside story, *Billy Budd* became a way for Melville to memorialize in fiction his lost shipmates, many of whom had surely died unknown to fame, while most of the survivors must have lived out their long lives more obscurely even than Melville, who had once experienced all but the highest literary fame and whose reputation was belatedly reviving. It became fitting that Melville blur fictional record and factual record by dedicating his inside fictional narrative to his real comrade, "Jack Chase / Englishman / Wherever that great heart may now be / Here on Earth or harbored in Paradise."

Hayford and Sealts show that when Melville began the headnote to "Billy in the Darbies," he had in mind "neither the plot of a novel nor any one of the characters as they later emerged" (2). What he had, the editors show, "was a short composition in both prose and verse that in its complete form ran to perhaps five or six leaves" (2). It concerned a sailor named Billy, apparently guilty of mutiny, who falls into a reverie on the eve of his execution. The editors say tersely, "The prose sketch and ballad thus placed a character in a situation but stopped short of telling a story" (2). Writing this story never, as far as we know, became obsessive with Melville for any prolonged period, although portions of it (the Nelson chapter, in particular) recurrently and strenuously demanded attention: the story was one of several literary projects which he was pushing forward on, concurrently, as his declining strength allowed, and not necessarily the project he considered most important. (If it had been the most important thing he was working on he might have finished it and printed it in 1887, or 1888, or any later time up till his death.)

In early 1886 Melville had been retired only a few weeks when news arrived of the death of his second son, Stanwix, in San Francisco, and before the year was out Melville's sensitive and deeply sympathetic brother-in-law, John C. Hoadley, had also died. Yet the year brought letters and gifts from English admirers, and the accidental acquaintance of a young American artist, Peter Toft, who gave Melville watercolors, one illustrating a scene from his work of 1854, "The Encantadas," and whom Melville entrusted with a letter to deliver to W. Clark Russell in England. From Russell in the summer of 1886 came this testimony: "Your reputation here is very great. It is hard to meet a man whose opinion as a reader is worth having who does not speak of your works in such terms as he might hesitate to employ with all his patriotism, towards many renowned English writers" (Metcalf 272). Hayford and Sealts show that during 1886-87 the headnote to the poem developed into a narrative about Billy Budd the Handsome Sailor, but they could not date particular stages in that development by study of the manuscript; the situation is complicated by the fact that 1887 is a year with little known documentation of *any* of Melville's activities.

In 1888 one of the leading literary men of the new generation, Edmund C. Stedman, succeeded in breaking through Melville's isolation, and Stedman's son Arthur became something of an intimate of the old man. Early in the year Melville sailed on his last sea-voyage, a winter trip to the Bermudas, and on his return his mind seems to have been on poetry more than his story of Billy Budd. Around the end of March he wrote Russell to ask permission to dedicate a volume of poems to him, *John Marr*, and the selection and polishing of the poems and the laborious composition of the dedication surely account for the press of time he mentioned in April to young Billson. Hayford and Sealts show that Melville seems to have made a fair copy of the *Billy Budd* story early in 1888 while he was "selecting and engrossing the poems he would include in *John Marr and Other Sailors*" (6)—a fair copy running only to a little more than seventy leaves. What had been a "situation" (Hayford and Sealts's description [p. 2] of the work when it ran only to some five or six pages, including the ballad) gradually became a narrative. In this phase the subplot involving Claggart's spies was developed, and Claggart himself "had come to occupy the foreground of the work" (6).

The death of his brother-in-law George Griggs and his family's vacation notwithstanding, Melville saw the book of poems published in September 1888, in an edition of twenty-five copies, and he continued to do some research (on the historical background of the mutinies at the Nore and Spithead), and some writing, on *Billy Budd*, including, the editors speculate, the "digression on Nelson and Trafalgar that now constitutes Ch. 4" (7). By November 1888 (the editors determined from Melville's dating and their analysis of the inscription of the surviving leaves) the story was over 150 manuscript leaves long, and dealt with two main characters, Billy Budd, the first to be developed, and Claggart, the villainous master-at-arms, who falsely accuses Billy of mutiny. Now Billy's constitutional weakness, a stutter in emotional circumstances, prevents him from speaking, and he acts instead, striking the master-at-arms and killing him instantly. In this stage the captain played only a minor role. At the end of this version, *after* the ballad, Melville placed a news account (said to have been printed in a weekly naval chronicle of the time, a sort of newsletter) which ironically gets almost every detail wrong: Claggart is mourned as an innocent patriot and Billy is condemned as a depraved mutineer. In this phase, Hayford and Sealts show, the captain's role was so small that "only a few leaves stood between the killing of Claggart and the beginning of the ballad" (2).

On 16 November 1888 Melville set about tidying the story, and "on later leaves he noted the dates 'Nov 17' and 'Nov 18' at intervals that probably marked a day's copy work" (7). At this stage, Hayford and Sealts show, he added "the Negro sailor and characterizations of Captain Graveling and Lieutenant Ratcliffe" to chapter 1 (7-8), and revised his sketch of the Dansker in chapter 9 (8). He also, on second thoughts, removed the section on Nelson and put it in a folder. Hayford and Sealts emphasize that the revisions at this stage concerned only the first ten chapters, and that what followed was the ballad and then the garbled news account. After the news account Melville added "a one-sentence coda to the entire narrative: 'Here ends a story not unwarranted by what sometimes happens in this [one undeciphered word: "incongruous"?] world of ours—Innocence and infamy, spiritual depravity and fair repute'" (8). At this time, then, there was hardly any possibility of questioning what the story meant: Melville had given it as unambiguous a moral as Henry Wadsworth Longfellow had ever placed at the end of a poem.

It turned out that "Here ends" did not long remain true, for Melville's recopying and tidying up merged into a third phase of development. In the months after November 1888, Hayford and Sealts show, Melville was led into revisions in which the narrative took on new philosophical and dramatic dimensions and grew to some 350 manuscript pages. In this period Melville wrote material to stand between the killing of Claggart and the ballad: "Billy's trial, Vere's long speech to the court, and the dramatized execution and related episodes intervene" (2). Melville also wrote a new analysis of Vere's character to be placed in chapters before Claggart is killed. In this stage of the story's evolution Melville developed the character of Captain Vere as a man with a nature as exceptional as Billy's own, one capable of embodying the conflicts between Nature and civilization, justice and law, intuition and duty. By the time Melville had so developed Vere, the news account and the coda he had written earlier did not in any sense round off or close off the later-written dramatic scenes between Vere and Billy and they did not resolve the issues raised by the fact that Billy was both innocent and guilty. Melville recognized something of the anomaly left on his hands, and when he ended the story at this third stage he arranged three "brief chapters" as (in his new words) "something in way of sequel" (128). The new chapter 28 reports that the injured and drugged Vere had murmured, just before his own death, the name of Billy Budd. Then as the next chapter Melville placed the news account (without the coda, since its ring of finality—"Here ends a story" [8]—made it unusable anywhere except at the *very* end, where it was no longer appropriate). The last chapter then consisted of two parts—first a somewhat rewritten version of the prose headnote about a sailor from Billy's own watch who wrote the poem "Billy in the Darbies," then the poem, slightly revised from the one which years before had been the first part of the whole work which Melville inscribed.

By 2 March 1889 Melville was far enough along to begin a major cleaning-up phase. Nevertheless, afterwards he was led into a final shift in which he removed or revised some of the passages where he had supported Vere's actions and replaced them with new passages that not only cast Vere's behavior into doubt but actually questioned Vere's sanity. The additions at this phase pushed the story in divergent directions, some older parts of it directing the reader to sympathize with Vere's actions, new parts holding his actions up to skeptical examination. Melville was still revising different parts of the manuscript when he died two and a half years later—but *not* doing anything so unambiguous as reworking pro-Vere passages into anti-Vere passages.

During this period there was no respite from grief, for Melville's older sister Helen (his devoted copyist for *Redburn* and *White-Jacket* during the summer of 1849) died in mid-December 1888, but familiar private grief mingled with public honor to which he had long been unaccustomed. W. Clark Russell published high praise of Melville ("one must search the pages of the Elizabethan dramatists to parallel" some utterances in *Moby-Dick*) in a Chicago paper (January 1889), and informed Melville that he was dedicating his new novel, *An Ocean Tragedy*, to him (it appeared early in 1890). Other praise reached America from abroad, and late in 1889 a Boston paper suggested that someone write Melville's life for the American Men of Letters series. From Nova Scotia in November 1889 the young professor Archibald MacMechan wrote a letter of high praise (calling Melville's earlier books "the most thoroughly New World product in all American literature"). In his eager admiration MacMechan asked Melville to write out information without realizing how exhausted the old man would have been by an attempt to answer him in any detail (Metcalf 276). That month the English Socialist H. S. Salt (already a great scholar of Thoreau) published an article on Melville in the *Scottish Art Review* and soon was in touch with him. Melville's health was noticeably declining by 5 December 1889, when he wrote MacMechan:

> But you do not know, perhaps, that I have entered my eighth decade. After twenty years nearly, as an outdoor Custom House officer, I have latterly come into possession of unobstructed leisure, but only just as, in the course of nature, my vigor sensibly declines. What little of it is left I husband for certain matters as yet incomplete, and which indeed may never be completed.

On 12 January 1890 Melville wrote Salt explaining that illness (probably an attack of erysipelas) had prevented an earlier reply.

Early in the year he was absorbed with arranging poems for *As They Fell*. Presumably he intended a private publication like that of *John Marr*, but he did not push this collection to publication. He may not have worked much on *Billy Budd*, either, although at the end of May he borrowed a minor source, Douglas Jerrold's *The Mutiny at the Nore*, from a library. Instead, he gave priority to another collection of poems. During the year evidence of the growing interest in England continued to reach Melville, and (fueled by English interest) American papers continued their occasional articles on him. Late in the year, as soon as winter came, he sickened, and developed a bad cough.

About the first of January 1891 Melville was taken sick after he walked too far "in a bitter cold air." In the night he had "dizziness or vertigo" which alarmed his doctor, but he improved enough to resume intermittent work at his desk (Metcalf 280). Finishing *Billy Budd* now may have taken on a higher order of priority than Melville had given it before. On 19 April 1891, he recopied at least part of the poem "Billy in the Darbies" and wrote after it, "End of Book," perhaps confirming that the poem was to end the work rather than the news account, or perhaps recording a temporary impression that the work was completed. In May the publisher De Vinne got out Melville's second collection of poems in two years, *Timoleon*, dedicated to his "countryman," the artist Elihu Vedder. In August he was working again on "Weeds & Wildings," for then he composed a dedication to "Winnefred" (his wife).

All the time he was working on *Billy Budd* Melville was old and tiring, and most of the time he was perceptibly weakening when not observably sick. Even as he began work on the prose headnote to "Billy in the Darbies," he was aware of a further decline in his physical strength, and that decline meant that he faltered his way into the story as he wrote the opening two chapters. As he worked his way further into it he gained remarkably in coherence and in a new concentration of literary powers, but (long out of the habit of writing professionally) he found it hard to keep the manuscript legible even when his thought was unfaltering. As far as we know Melville never had thought of buying and mastering one of the newfangled typewriters, and now he resorted (as writers who compose in longhand still do) to various awkward strategies to avoid copying clean parts over. Hayford and Sealts describe his habit of cutting off parts of leaves and pinning them (sometimes, later on, gluing them) to full-sized leaves: "Some of these part-leaves bear passages Melville salvaged by clipping them from *earlier* leaves merely to avoid copying them; these we call 'clips.' Others bear revisions or insertions *later* than the copy stage of the leaves to which they are fastened; these we call 'patches'" (225).

Each attempt to get the story into fair copy required a new concentration of physical and intellectual energies. In Melville's state of declining energy some thoughts could not be completed, or if worked out in the mind were not put down fully on paper, and some tasks which he keenly perceived as essential to complete were never carried out. Sometimes Melville made matters worse, as when he belatedly tried to straighten out the number and personnel needed for a court martial, and although he jotted down some housekeeping notations about the need to eliminate inconsistencies and to plant necessary information at the right place, he did not manage to achieve all that he saw needed to be done: for example, he reminded himself that he needed to "Speak of the fight & death of Captain Vere" (420) before chapter 29 could make sense, and did so, but he did not live to handle other anomalous details. He may well not have noticed some loose ends which patient students of the manuscript can now discern. He needed help, and if his wife had been free or had felt free to follow after him at every stage, copying after him, as she and his sisters Augusta and Helen had once done, then he might have reworked all the parts of the story to something like an equal degree of finish and might have taken care of all the details that obtruded on his consciousness but were too awkward or too difficult or too baffling for him to resolve them at any given time. When he died on 28 September 1891, Melville was still revising the manuscript of *Billy Budd, Sailor*, not having resolved the direction in which Vere's characterization was to go, and leaving other minor contradictions. We do not honor Melville by pretending *Billy Budd* is complete and perfect: to close our eyes to the relation between artistic imperfection and failing health is to dehumanize the creative process and the created product.

*Chapter Four*

---

# Preservation and Transcription

---

THE DISHEARTENING EXPERIENCES OF THE FIRST-TIME EDITOR WHOM
Melville invented to try to shepherd the "Burgundy Club" material into print pretty obviously reflect Melville's bemusement with
his own situation around the time of his retirement or in the years
just before his death. In old age he found himself, once again,
about to venture into print, despite the disaster of *Clarel*. For all
we know, the rueful self-satirizing in "House of the Tragic Poet"
directly reflected Melville's decision after his retirement to put
some of his poetry and other unfinished work into shape fit to
print, and the related decision to pay for the publication himself
and not to subject the volumes to the full glare of journalistic
publicity. The reasonable assumption is that the ballad about Billy
Budd would have gone into *John Marr and Other Sailors* if Melville
had finished it up merely as a poem, and the evidence of the
manuscript of *Billy Budd* is strong that Melville was preparing it
as a book to be published, not merely writing for his own bemusement. As we have seen, he repeatedly attempted to start over and
make a fair copy of the entire manuscript (only to have each attempt frustrated by his being drawn into new phases of composition). Furthermore, when it seemed that he might be nearing
completion his wife began to make "slight secretarial corrections"
(7) like those she made on parts of the manuscripts for the *Timoleon* volume. These were her preparatory marks to keep her from
blundering unnecessarily once she proceeded to copy a manuscript
out for the printer, but in the case of *Billy Budd* before she could
actually start copying Melville took back the manuscript in order

to make further expansions and revisions. What form the publication might have taken is doubtful. Melville had been humiliated by the fate of *Clarel*, published by Putnam's in 1876 at his own expense (the costs being paid for by a legacy from his uncle Peter Gansevoort). Stuck with unsold copies of the two-volume poem, Putnam's required Melville's assent to disposing of two boxes of the volumes, and may even have billed him for the cost of getting rid of the volumes for him. There was to be no more such humiliation, for Melville had *John Marr* and *Timoleon* privately printed, in editions of twenty-five copies each, for personal distribution to family and a few friends. (De Vinne, the printer of the first of these volumes, and Caxton, the printer of the second, were often used by well-to-do writers for fine private printing.) It is likely that if Melville had finished the story early in 1891, while he still had some strength, he would have prepared it for printing by an American house specializing in fine printing. Other possibilities might have opened up. If Melville had lived a little longer his English reputation might have been so high that one of his admirers could have persuaded a London publisher to take an amazing prize, a new piece of fiction by the man who became famous half a century before for living among the cannibals.

Nothing so dramatic happened. After Melville's death in September 1891, his widow enlisted her young neighbor Arthur Stedman, son of the prominent Wall Street man and litterateur Edmund C. Stedman, who had met Melville in 1888, as a sort of literary executor for her husband's books. Through Arthur Stedman's efforts four of Melville's early works were reprinted in both the United States and England in 1892. In writing his biographical and critical account of Melville's career as an introduction to the first of these volumes, *Typee*, Stedman had access to Melville's papers, even to his accounts with his publishers. The Stedman edition was not a success, partly because of the Wall Street Panic of 1893. Afterwards, Stedman endured some impoverished and embittering years in London which left him with no interest in advancing Melville's reputation. What is baffling is that Stedman during his task of getting out new editions of four of Melville's early works did not, as far as we know, ever make any comment on the *Billy Budd* manuscript, much less do what one would think the most obvious thing: transcribe and publish it not only in order to preserve it and give it a chance for fame in the world but also as an effective ploy for advertising the other volumes, since one way of guaranteeing that attention will be paid to reprints of old books is to accompany the long-familiar with the absolutely fresh. In *The Early Lives of Melville* (Madison: University of Wisconsin Press, 1974) Merton M. Sealts, Jr., puzzles over the fact that in newspaper articles and in his long introduction to his edition of *Typee* Stedman made no mention at all of *Billy Budd*:

> He [Stedman] mentions the privately printed *John Marr* and *Timoleon* but takes no cognizance of other literary work done in Melville's last years that was left unpublished at the time of his death. . . . Unless he was simply unaware of the body of late manuscripts, it seems strange that he did not mention or quote other verse—from "Weeds and Wildings" in particular—in any of his essays. And in view of his expressed conviction that new publications are the key to sustaining public interest in an author, it is strange too that as Melville's literary executor he did not prepare *Billy Budd* for publication, either in one of the magazines like *Harper's* or the *Century* or as a separate volume, since Melville himself would presumably have wanted to see it in print, with *John Marr* and *Timoleon*, if he had lived. Did Stedman ever examine the *Billy Budd* manuscript? If he did, was he baffled by Melville's cabalistic hand—which Mrs. Melville could of course have helped him to interpret if both were so inclined? Or did Stedman, with his penchant for Melville's autobiographical writings, simply pass it over as a piece of minor historical fiction, more suitable for Clark Russell than for Melville, or too "rugged and mystical" for *Typee*-lovers to enjoy? We shall probably never know. (62-63)

So much new information has come to light in the last decade that one dares to hope we will learn more about this odd circumstance, but Sealts is justified in his conclusion that we shall "probably never know."

Melville's granddaughter Eleanor Melville Metcalf in her *Herman Melville: Cycle and Epicycle* is the source for the only known description of the way the manuscript of *Billy Budd* was treated in the first ten or fifteen years after his death:

> Among my most cherished girlhood memories were the visits made to my grandmother's apartment [in the Florence]—most

especially when my grandmother, in the early years of the twentieth century, invited for the evening our mutual good friend,
the Reverend Samuel Henry Bishop, a man of unusual integrity,
good mind, and more than ordinary sensitivity, in order to enlist
his interest in her husband's books and manuscripts.

We would sit in the library, surrounded by the remaining
books of Melville's collection, himself looking down on us from
his place over the white marble mantelpiece, as alive as the artist
Eaton portrayed him, the precious box of manuscripts on the
same table where he used to write. While "Billy Budd" and
fugitive, discarded, or rewritten poems were inspected, I listened
with ignorant enthusiasm to their conversation. (289)

Born early in 1882, Mrs. Metcalf was a young woman at the turn
of the century, but may well have kept a polite and deferential
reserve around the minister, who is the first person outside the
family known to have seen any of *Billy Budd*.

As far as we now know, the second outsider to see the *Billy
Budd* manuscript was Frank Jewett Mather, Jr., a young art historian who had become a Melville-lover in 1891 and who, as he
recalled, by accident met E. C. Stedman (Arthur's father) in 1902
(perhaps an error for 1906, after Mrs. Melville's death in July) and
received from him an introduction to Melville's daughter Elizabeth, who after her mother's death still lived in the Florence, "one
of the pioneer apartment houses of Manhattan," surrounded by
"her father's effects"—"silvery prints after Poussin and Claude on
the walls," the remnants of Melville's library on shelves, and "a
japanned tin cake-box which was stuffed with Melville's archives,"
including *Billy Budd*. She opened the box before his "delighted
eyes" and let him glance over "the unpublished manuscript of
*Billy Budd*" and take notes from some diaries, so that he knew
himself "in the position of a discoverer of hidden treasure"
("Reminiscences of a Melvillian," *"Moby-Dick" as Doubloon*, ed.
Hershel Parker and Harrison Hayford [New York: Norton, 1970]:
181). Mather needed an advance of around $500 in order to sup-
port him during his research and composition of a biography of
Melville, but in November 1906, Ferris Greenslet, the editor at
Houghton Mifflin, refused him any advance at all in view of Melville's low reputation, and Mather abandoned his plans.

Melville's daughter Elizabeth died in 1908, two years after her
mother, and Melville's literary papers went to his younger daughter

Frances Melville Thomas, then living in South Orange, New Jersey; she stored the box "most of the time in the attic" where the contents survived the vicissitudes in weather until she passed the documents along to her oldest daughter Eleanor, apparently in the centenary of Melville's birth, 1919. This gift was altogether appropriate, Frances knew, for her own mother, Melville's widow, had instilled in Eleanor the duty to become the guardian of Herman Melville's fame. The papers were still preserved in the japanned tin box (a "bread box," Mrs. Metcalf emphatically said, not a "trunk"—or a cake-box), now in the Melville Room in the Berkshire Athenaeum in Pittsfield. As far as we know the next person outside the family to see it was Raymond Weaver, a Columbia graduate student, set to work on Melville by Carl Van Doren. In 1919 Weaver was given the name of the librarian at the Berkshire Athenaeum as a possible source of information about Melville. At his suggestion, Weaver wrote to Melville's niece, Mrs. William Morewood, who was summering at Arrowhead, Melville's old home. The reply to Weaver, dated 9 July 1919, came from Melville's daughter Frances Melville Thomas, in Edgertown:

> I am quite willing to have you write a life of my father, Herman Melville, but fear I can not help you very much. I should be obliged to put the matter in my daughter[']s hands, as I am in ill health, and have serious troubles with my eyes.

Weaver arranged to meet Eleanor Thomas Metcalf at a station in a western suburb of Boston in August 1919. The following is from a later handwritten account, now in Weaver's papers in the Columbia University Library:

> Mrs. Metcalf herself was their [i.e., there]. And [An] English-looking woman, with flat heels, a rain-coat . . . . She had a taxi. "This weather is enough to provoke conversation" she said at once on the way to her home; "but you dont want to talk about the weather. So I'll tell you at once the worst—though I trust you as a gentleman as to what you'll ever publish."
>
> She said: "You say, in your *Nation* article, that Melville was happily married. He wasn't."
>
> And before the short ride to her house was over, I felt that Melville was a man of even deeper secrets than I had expected.
>
> We opened the trunk of manuscript—as I've recounted in an article that follows.

Always, it rained.

The "article that follows" (presumably printed) does not in fact accompany this manuscript, and the Northwestern-Newberry editors of Melville have not yet discovered what Weaver referred to. Presumably, a colorful story is yet to be located.

We know, however, that at the time Weaver was not impressed with the manuscript fiction that Mrs. Metcalf showed him. In his *Herman Melville: Mariner and Mystic* (New York: Doran, 1921) he printed Archibald MacMechan's request for information as well as Melville's polite explanation that he was husbanding his strength for "certain matters as yet incomplete, and which indeed may never be completed." Weaver then commented:

> Melville was using his "unobstructed leisure" in a return to the writing of prose. Ten prose sketches and a novel were the result. But the result is not distinguished. The novel, *Billy Budd*, is built around the character of Jack Chase, the "Handsome Sailor." In the character of Billy Budd, Melville attempts to portray the native purity and nobility of the uncorrupted man. Melville spends elaborate pains in analysing "the mystery of iniquity," and in celebrating by contrast the god-like beauty of body and spirit of his hero. Billy Budd, by his heroic guilelessness is, like an angel of vengeance, precipitated into manslaughter; and for his very righteousness he is hanged. *Billy Budd*, finished within a few months before the end of Melville's life, would seem to teach that though the wages of sin is death, that [*sic*] sinners and saints alike toil for a common hire. In *Billy Budd* the orphic sententiousness is gone, it is true. But gone also is the brisk lucidity, the sparkle, the verve. Only the disillusion abided with him to the last. (381)

This left-handed recommendation was enough, it turned out, to cause Melville's British admirer Michael Sadleir to appeal to Weaver to transcribe the manuscript so that it could fill out volume 13 of the Constable "Standard Edition" of Melville's *Complete Works* (1924). Weaver was simply not the man to spend years transcribing and working out the sequence of composition of a single manuscript, no matter how much historical interest it might have (he may not have transcribed it all himself, for a decade later he acknowledged that his 1935 edition of Melville's 1856-57 journal was based on a transcription by someone else, Gerald Crona).

He meant well, but he clearly saw his addition to the canon of Melville's works as not much more than an advertising bonus for the new collected edition.

In the late 1950s and early 1960s two scholars, Harrison Hayford and Merton M. Sealts, Jr., devoted to the manuscript the sort of study that it deserved, and showed that Weaver had included some discarded passages in the text (according one passage rejected from a late chapter the quite false honor of being the preface). As we have seen, Mrs. Melville had not been privy to all the stages of Melville's progress on *Billy Budd*. After his death when she sorted through the manuscript and related papers she queried of three leaves (in the Hayford-Sealts numbering, leaves 358-60), "Preface for Billy Budd?" (377). She did not realize that Melville had discarded them and she wondered, sensibly enough, whether or not anything starting "The year 1797" could have been meant as the preface, for Melville had often given his books prefaces. In his efforts to copy out the manuscript for printing in the Constable Edition Weaver had made the understandable mistake of ignoring her question mark and printing the passage as "Preface." Hayford and Sealts also showed that, all along, particular words were not Melville's but merely Weaver's best guess at what was in the manuscript, and that Weaver had casually brought Melville's wording and punctuation toward conformity with what he thought was desirable usage. He even gave to the work a title Melville had tried and rejected, *Billy Budd, Foretopman*. And simply by creating the impression that Melville had completed *Billy Budd*, Weaver set up false expectations which still bedevil readers of the book.

Readers always pick up a printed and bound literary work expecting that it will be, at the very least, coherent and complete. Any reader encountering a "Preface" at the beginning of a book will accord it special attention, since by their nature prefaces are supposed not just to ease the reader's way into the rest of the story but also to do more than that—to give the reader clues as to how to interpret a more than usually complicated story. Readers of the Weaver text saw the story as very much a historical novel. When they opened to the story in the Constable edition, on the verso (the left-hand page) was the second (last) page of the table of contents, and on the recto (the right-hand page) was a title: "BILLY BUDD, FORETOPMAN / WHAT BEFELL HIM IN THE

YEAR OF / THE GREAT MUTINY, Etc." Toward the bottom of the page Weaver printed three lines:

> Friday, Nov. 16, 1888—begun.
> Revision begun—March 2, 1889.
> Finished—April 19, 1891.

Weaver had mistaken a date Melville began making a fair copy for the date the first work on the story was started, and he had recorded the "finished" date without realizing that Melville's "End of Book / April 19$^{th}$ 1891" (inscribed below the ballad) may have meant only that the ballad was definitely to conclude the book, instead of the news account that had once stood at the end, and without realizing that even if the notation meant Melville thought he was "finished" in fact he had kept on working beyond that date. On the *next* page Weaver printed the dedication to Jack Chase, Englishman, taking ten lines, and the facing right-hand page began with a conspicuous title, "PREFACE," followed by words which certainly looked mighty like a preface:

> The year 1797, the year of this narrative, belongs to a period which, as every thinker now feels, involved a crisis for Christendom, not exceeded in its undetermined momentousness at the time by any other era whereof there is record. The opening proposition made by the Spirit of that Age [Weaver footnoted here the information that Melville had written then had crossed out these words: "was one hailed by the noblest men of it. Even the dry tinder of Wordsworth took fire."], involved a rectification of the Old World's hereditary wrongs. In France, to some extent, this was bloodily effected. But what then? Straightway the Revolution itself became a wrongdoer, one more oppressive than the kings. Under Napoleon it enthroned upstart kings, and initiated that prolonged agony of continual war whose final throe was Waterloo. During those years not the wisest could have foreseen that the outcome of all would be what to some thinkers apparently it has since turned out to be, a political advance along nearly the whole line for Europeans.
>
> Now, as elsewhere hinted, it was something caught from the Revolutionary Spirit that at Spithead emboldened the man-of-war's men to rise against real abuses, long-standing ones, and afterwards at the Nore to make inordinate and aggressive demands, successful resistance to which was confirmed only when

the ringleaders were hung for an admonitory spectacle to the anchored fleet. Yet in a way analogous to the operation of the Revolution at large, the Great Mutiny, though by Englishmen naturally deemed monstrous at the time, doubtless gave the first latent prompting to most important reforms in the British Navy. (3-4)

The last six lines of the "preface" ran over onto page 4, the rest of which was blank. On the facing recto there was a new title with a chapter number rather oddly placed between the title and what looked like a sort of new subtitle, three words in parentheses: "BILLY BUDD, FORETOPMAN / I / *(An inside Narrative)*." The following paragraph began in a way almost identical to the form we are now most familiar with: "In the time before steamships, or then more frequently than now, a stroller along the docks of any considerable seaport would occasionally have his attention arrested by a group of bronzed marines, man-of-war's men or merchant sailors in holiday attire ashore on liberty" (5). (Hayford and Sealts corrected "marines" to "mariners.")

In another editorial blunder Weaver put still more rejected words into the text. Toward the end of chapter 10, following the paragraph beginning "Now something such was Claggart" and concluding "'a depravity according to nature,'" he printed a paragraph Melville had deleted. (The place he printed it was a little ahead of the place it had actually occupied while it was in the manuscript.) Here is the passage as Weaver printed it:

Can it be this phenomenon, disowned or not acknowledged, that in some criminal cases puzzles the courts? For this cause have our juries at times not only to endure the prolonged contentions of lawyers with their fees, but also the yet more perplexing strife of the medical experts with theirs? But why leave it to them? Why not subpoena as well the clerical proficients? Their vocation bringing them into peculiar contact with so many human beings, and sometimes in their least guarded hour, in interviews very much more confidential than those of physician and patient; this would seem to qualify them to know something about those intricacies involved in the question of moral responsibility; whether in a given case, say, the crime proceeded from mania in the brain or rabies of the heart. As to any differences among themselves these clerical proficients might develop on the stand, these could hardly be greater than the direct contradictions exchanged between the remunerated medical experts. (46-47)

In Weaver's edition, two short paragraphs followed, the first beginning (47), "Dark sayings are these, some will say." Hayford and Sealts showed that the inclusion of this passage created strange redundancies, since Melville had used up, elsewhere in the manuscript, the essence of the lines he had discarded.

Readers of Weaver's text of *Billy Budd, Foretopman* were therefore confronted at the outset with words Melville had rejected from a late chapter of the manuscript but which could only be taken as a "Preface." There was no possible reason for skepticism about such a matter. Nor was there anything self-evidently wrong about the section on "lawyers, experts, clergy" which Melville had also deleted. These are only some of the invisible problems that misled the innocent reader of the Constable edition. Invisible in the elegantly printed lines of the text were Weaver's misreadings of Melville's very difficult handwriting, for ordinary readers take the words in a printed and bound book on faith as authorial. No reviewer mentioned textual oddities, and no reader wrote in to *Notes & Queries* to challenge individual words. The fact is that *Billy Budd, Foretopman* in the Weaver text was in most essentials a genuine Melvillean text, and it offered a powerful reading experience; lovers of Melville in 1924 could encounter something very close to what Melville had written so many years before. But the reading experience was subverted. There is nothing dishonorable in Weaver's merely doing the best he could, but by his hasty transcription and his misjudgments he created a situation in which readers formed quite erroneous opinions about the nature of *Billy Budd* and the function of some of its parts.

# *Billy Budd*:
# From *Foretopman* to *Sailor*

# Chapter Five

## The Dynamics of the Canonization
## of *Billy Budd, Foretopman*

MANY ACADEMIC THEORISTS ARE NOW FERVENTLY PROMULGATING A relativistic approach in which the canon of American literature is seen as the product of political, racial, and sexual (far more than aesthetic) forces and in which the idea of enduring aesthetic value is seen as an illusion fostered by (old, male, Caucasian) power-holding ideologues. Among the most forceful and plausible of these is Barbara Herrnstein Smith, the author of the provocative lead article, "Contingencies of Value," in the special issue of *Critical Inquiry* on canons (September 1983), an essay incorporated into her 1988 book of the same title. Some feminist theorists go so far as to say that for a given period—such as the biblical seven years—no one should teach a work by a man in any American literature course. Such ideologues grant Herman Melville no immunity from decanonization, even though he has already suffered an exclusion that lasted nearly a century. Remembering that white men have been silenced and ignored (as women of any race and as men of non-white races have been), all Melvilleans are keenly aware of how contingent the canon is on political, social, and economic forces, and tend to sympathize with anyone who reads earnestly and widely in all levels of literature with the goal of reassessing the canon. My evidence of how *Billy Budd, Foretopman* became a classic almost as soon as it was published in 1924, hyped by English literary men (not women) into the canon not just of American literature but of English-language literature, is the sort of story that invites misuse. Yet the story should interest anyone concerned with the dynamics of canonization, not just those anxious to impose their particular ideology upon literary history, and it suggests some thorny considerations not yet faced by recent theorists.

Since Melville did not enter the canon until the mid-twentieth century, American writers such as Stevens, Pound, Eliot, Fitzgerald, Faulkner, and Hemingway all read Bryant, Emerson, Hawthorne, Longfellow, Whittier, Poe, Holmes, and J. R. Lowell in school and not one of them, so far as we know, read anything by Melville in a formal educational setting such as high school and very few of them (only Faulkner?) encountered Melville in time to be influenced by him. Even in the 1930s and 1940s a major college textbook such as the Snyder and Snyder *A Book of American Literature* could be published without a single selection from Melville but with excellent representation of Whitman and (for the time) almost adequate representation of Dickinson, the two other great contemporaries of Melville who proved problematical to anthologizers. All that has changed, and along with many others I have anthologized Melville myself, in the *Norton Anthology of American Literature*, where the longest work by him is *Billy Budd, Sailor*. I don't stand ready to remove it because it was written by a man, or because it was written by an old white man in bad health, but there are intellectually and aesthetically honest ways in which one could challenge its present position in the canon of American literature. In the current political climate my evidence may be used in ways I would think inappropriate, but what follows is as honestly documented a story of the way the book entered the canon of great American literature as you have any right to expect from a professor who is old, male, and Caucasian-looking (though with close Cherokee and Choctaw ancestors).

Teachers tend to teach all of Melville in the pre–Civil War survey course, and when they write literary history they very rarely think of *Billy Budd* as a novel of the post–Gilded Age or the fin de siècle. They do not look for parallels to the mood of *Billy Budd* in some British and Continental writers Melville was reading as he wrote *Billy Budd*—James ("B. V.") Thomson's *City of Dreadful Night* or *Essays and Phantasies*, for instance, or Edward Fitz-Gerald's *Rubaiyat of Omar Khayyam*, or several novels by Honoré de Balzac, and they do not discuss *Billy Budd* along with American novels from the same period. Yet Melville was working on *Billy*

*Budd* at the same time that Henry James was writing *The Aspern Papers* (1888) and *The Tragic Muse* (1890), that W. D. Howells was writing *A Hazard of New Fortunes* (1890), that young Stephen Crane was writing *Maggie: A Girl of the Streets* (1893). Melville died less than a year before Mark Twain began drafting a much longer version of what he serialized in 1893-94 as *Pudd'nhead Wilson*.

In terms of publishing history, to be sure, *Billy Budd* has nothing to do with works of the 1880s, 1890s, 1900s, 1910s, or the first years after World War I. *Billy Budd, Foretopman* was published (first in England, not the United States) in mid-1924, so it was a near-contemporary of D. H. Lawrence's *Kangaroo* (1923), of F. Scott Fitzgerald's *The Great Gatsby* (1925), of Ernest Hemingway's *In Our Time* (1925; shorter Paris edition, with lowercase title, 1924), and of William Faulkner's *Soldiers' Pay* (1926). Naturally we have trouble gaining perspective on a story published so out of its own time, and even out of its own country. A good way of focusing on the situation is to realize that when D. H. Lawrence drafted his book on American literature in the late 1910s he was one of the new British enthusiasts for *Moby-Dick*, but he thought of Melville still as the author of *Typee*, *Omoo*, and *Moby-Dick*. That is, he was following the judgment of the late 1840s and 1850s that Melville's first two books were of more interest than most of his subsequent ones; the only difference was that he was following the judgment of the 1880s and 1890s in according the highest position to one of those later books, *Moby-Dick*. When Lawrence published his *Studies in Classic American Literature* in 1923, only a few people knew that *Billy Budd* existed; Lawrence himself had probably never heard of it; as it happened, his friend John Middleton Murry was to orchestrate its reception internationally.

Now Murry is remembered, if at all, as the husband of Katherine Masefield and intimate of Lawrence (who drew from him the portrait of Gerald Crich in *Women in Love*) and Frieda Lawrence (briefly her lover). He was a latecomer to Melville but because of his position at the *Nation and Athenaeum* an extremely important admirer. What provoked his and his colleague H. M. Tomlinson's interest was the Oxford World's Classics edition of *Moby-Dick* (1920), which just missed appearing in the centennial of Melville's birth, 1919. In the "Historical Note" to the Northwestern-Newberry edition of *Moby-Dick* (1988) I described the parts Murry and Tomlinson played in bringing the "Melville Revival" to fever-pitch:

> A copy [of the 1920 Oxford edition of *Moby-Dick*] caused such consternating ecstasy in the office of *The Nation* that two years later the sea-novelist H. M. Tomlinson dated the Melville revival from its publication. Tomlinson was recalling that early in 1921, as a staff member of the *Nation* just before its merger with the *Athenaeum*, he had bought a copy of the World's Classics edition and written about it, "incoherently indeed, but with signs of emotion as intense and as pleasingly uncouth as Man Friday betrayed at the sight of his long-lost father." While the editor, John Middleton Murry, was "struggling" with Tomlinson's article, "and wondering what the deuce it could mean," there arrived from Augustine Birrell, an enthusiast for many years (put on to Melville by Sir Alfred Lyall), a review of the World's Classics edition "marked on the outside 'Urgent,' and on the inner scroll of the MS. itself, 'A Rhapsody.'" Having read Birrell's tribute ("The two striking features of this book, after allowing for the fact that it is a work of genius and therefore *sui generis*, are, as it appears to me, its most amazing eloquence, and its mingling of an ever-present romanticism of style with an almost savage reality of narrative"), Murry himself read the book and reported: "I hereby declare, being of sane intellect, that since letters began there never was such a book, and that the mind of man is not constructed so as to produce such another; that I put its author with Rabelais, Swift, Shakespeare, and other minor and disputable worthies; and that I advise any adventurer of the soul to go at once into the morose and prolonged retreat necessary for its deglutition." From this time Tomlinson and Murry used the columns of the *Nation and Athenaeum* in promoting the reputation of Melville and his masterpiece. (750-51)

One of the ways Tomlinson, Murry, and others promoted the Revival was in repeatedly demanding that some American provide them with a biography of Melville.

When Raymond Weaver's *Herman Melville: Mariner and Mystic* was published in 1921 there was dismay in London literary circles, for it was plain that Weaver's derivative, poorly researched, disproportioned, and aesthetically insensitive book would provide little information to rely on and would actively prevent another

American from undertaking a more conscientious study—at a time when many were still alive who had known Melville, and might have been interviewed. The great English bookman Michael Sadleir showed that the British could at least do Melville the honor of a full collected edition. During late 1922 and throughout 1923 the publication of successive volumes in Sadleir's Constable Edition of *The Works of Herman Melville* evoked many long articles appraising Melville's literary oeuvre. The number and the scope of these general essays make it clear that magazine and newspaper editors had no notion that they ought to reserve their comprehensive essays until the publication of the last volumes, not originally announced for inclusion in the set. The essays seem to have been written in apparent unawareness that a story called *Billy Budd* existed in any form, although some of the writers may have seen Weaver's slighting comments on it in his biography. There was no mention of *Billy Budd* in these self-conscious summations not just on the one book, *Moby-Dick*, which had been wildly praised during several recent years, but on other books as well, particularly *Pierre*, which incited enthusiastic and sometimes ecstatic admiration in London.

Sadleir was enlarging the announced scope of the Constable Edition when he enlisted Raymond Weaver to transcribe any significant unpublished writings to fill out volume 13. Published in mid-1924, *Billy Budd, Foretopman* was perceived at once in London as a wonderful bonus bestowed upon those enthusiasts of *Moby-Dick* who had in the previous few years revived Melville's fame in a most astonishing way. Murry got the privilege of reviewing *Billy Budd* in the influential *Times Literary Supplement*, in an essay called "Herman Melville's Silence" (10 July 1924); it was anonymous, according to long-standing policy, but authorship was always an open secret among the cognoscenti. Although he had read in *Battle-Pieces* and even had read a good deal of *Clarel*, Murry talked repeatedly of Melville's "long silence" after *Pierre* (1852). His reading of *Pierre* is directly relevant to his reading of *Billy Budd, Foretopman*:

> Let those who are persuaded that a novel is a good story and nothing more avoid "Pierre." But those who feel that the greatest novels are something quite different from a good story should seek it out: to them it will be strange and fascinating, and they

will understand why its outward semblance is clumsy and puer-
ile. Melville is trying to reveal a mystery; he is trying to show
that the completely good man is doomed to complete disaster on
earth, and he is trying to show at the same time that this must
be so, and that it ought to be so. The necessity of that "ought
to be so" can be interpreted in two ways: as Melville calls them,
horologically or chronometrically. Horologically—that is, estimated by our local and earthly timepieces—the disaster of the
good ought to be so, because there is no room for unearthly
perfection on earth; chronometrically—that is, estimated by the
unvarying recorder of the absolute—it ought to be so, because it
is a working out, a manifestation, of the absolute, though hidden, harmony of the ideal and the real. In other words, Melville
was trying to reveal anew the central mystery of the Christian
religion.

He did not succeed.

In Murry's view, Melville's silence was broken only by *Billy Budd*,
and therefore the story is to be attended to with awe:

> With the mere fact of the long silence in our minds we could not
> help regarding "Billy Budd" as the last will and spiritual testa-
> ment of a man of genius. We could not help expecting this, if
> we have any imaginative understanding. Of course, if we are
> content to dismiss in our minds, if not in our words, the man of
> genius as mad, there is no need to trouble. Some one is sure to
> have told us that "Billy Budd," like "Pierre," is a tissue of naiv-
> ety and extravagance: that will be enough. And, truly, "Billy
> Budd" *is* like "Pierre"—startlingly like. Once more Melville is
> telling the story of the inevitable and utter disaster of the good
> and trying to convey to us that this must be so and ought to be
> so—chronometrically and horologically. He is trying, as it were
> with his final breath, to reveal the knowledge that has been
> haunting him—that these things must be so and not otherwise.

Murry recounted the plot and quoted the four paragraphs describing Billy's execution (ending with the motionless pinioned figure).
For him, the story was a revelation of a mystery: "It was Melville's
final word, worthy of him, indisputably a passing beyond the ni-
hilism of 'Moby Dick' to what may seem to some simple and
childish, but will be to others wonderful and divine."

Murry's essay, slightly expanded (and with a quotation slightly
shortened) was republished under his name in the *New York Times*

*Book Review* (10 August 1924), headlined "Herman Melville, Who Could Not Surpass Himself / Complete Works of a Writer of Colossal Vision—After 'Moby Dick' He Had Nothing More to Say." The headline (surely supplied at the *Times*) shows pretty clearly how far behind the British the Americans were in coming to terms with Melville. Despite any muffling effects of the headline, Murry had the chance to set the tone for the reception of *Billy Budd* in both countries, in the most important reviewing organs in London and in New York.

Murry also published in the London magazine *The Adelphi* (August 1924) a little essay entitled "Quo Warranto?" It contained a remarkable comment on the importance of *Billy Budd* to him personally. At the outset he explained that a writer in the *Spectator* on 17 May 1924 had launched an attack against *The Adelphi*, then he corrected himself: "To be accurate, his anathema was levelled less against the magazine than against myself and Mr. D. H. Lawrence. It was a pretty piece of invective, in the main personal. Mr. Lawrence and myself were convicted of dishonesty and vanity, above all of vanity" (185). From this beginning Murry proceeded to write a Laurentian history of his soul, a history that led ultimately, in his case, to Jesus. In this journey Melville was a deeply felt presence:

> When great spirits touch a certain depth of knowledge of human life, this is the path they follow,—the path that leads to a new comprehension of the mystery of Christ. When in a writer's work I am thrilled by contact with this depth of knowledge of human life, I am certain that I shall find him at the last following this predestined path. Such a profound depth of knowledge I found in Herman Melville's "Moby Dick"—knowledge of the same order that is in "Lear" and "Macbeth." The end, I said to myself, will be the same. At that time I could not prove it. Melville's later works are rare, and two years back they were impossible for me to obtain. I had to bide my time until a few months ago when four supplementary volumes to the collected edition of Melville's works were published—volumes which contained the unprocurable and "unintelligible" works of his long period of silence. I turned to the last of these, an unpublished story, written with pains and care, immediately before his death—his final word, his spiritual testament. It con-

tained precisely what I had expected: a deliberate effort to restate
the mystery of Christ—the catastrophe of the utterly pure and
good, and its complete triumph in the very moment of death.
(193-94)

This astoundingly personal account deserves very close attention,
for better than any other evidence known, it suggests the intensity
of power the rediscovered Melville had over many of the most
earnest and most active literary people in England at the time of
the Revival—and people of all generations, not just those of Murry's and Lawrence's age. (I will recur to Murry's sense of the dis-
paraging term "unintelligible" for contrast with my literal use of
it later in this section.) Murry's idiosyncratic passion fueled the
canonization of *Billy Budd* in Great Britain and in the United
States. *Billy Budd* within months of its publication was canonized—was placed among the most precious of the sacred texts in
the English language, among those few which can effect transform-
ing confirmations and inspirations in lives of individual readers.

When *Billy Budd* appeared, the now-obscure English poet and
general literary man John Freeman was already gathering material
for a study of Melville which was by the mere fact of its existence a
remarkable tribute, for it was to go in the English Men of Letters
Series. (A charming oddity is that the British so frankly claimed
Melville in the 1920s that he still appears now and then in the
*Times Literary Supplement* listed with "other" British writers. The
British absorbed Melville into a literary tradition in a way Americans still have not done.) In his little critical biography (London:
Macmillan, 1926) Freeman refers to *Billy Budd* at first mention as
"a belated brief masterpiece" which Melville finished just before
his death (33). His second reference to it is as "a marvelous prose
lyric or lyrical narrative" (68). Chapter 7 bears an astonishing title:
"*Moby-Dick* and *Billy Budd*."

Wholly unknown to the public until mid-1924, *Billy Budd* now
in 1926 had joint billing with the book which had just barely been
firmly established as a literary masterpiece. Ever since the 1880s
one brilliant reader after another had been saying that *Moby-Dick*
was the great Melville work, not *Typee*—and now in the great
acceleration of Melville's fame in the Revival Freeman did not have
to argue his evaluation of *Moby-Dick* or even his placing the newly

born *Billy Budd* in a chapter title with it. Freeman began with grand-scale ranking:

> If it seems fantastic to compare *Moby-Dick* with Milton's *Paradise Lost* and assert a parallel conception in each, it will seem fantastic to say that in a shorter story, *Billy Budd*, may be found another *Paradise Regained*.
>
> Like *Moby-Dick* this late and pure survival of Melville's genius has a double interest, the interest of story and the interest of psychology. (131)

The pages which follow sympathetically summarize the story, concluding with the whole of the execution scene, already given currency throughout the English-reading world by Murry; the last quoted paragraph is the same one about the motionless "pinioned figure."

Then Freeman moved into evaluative commentary on the execution which deserves very close reading, and which will require, afterwards, a pause to deal with something problematical:

> Exaltation of spirit redeems such a scene from burdens which otherwise might appear too painful to be borne. And beyond this, it is innocence that is vindicated, more conspicuously in death than it could be in life. Melville's MS. contains a note in his own hand—"A story not unwarranted by what happens in this incongrous world of ours—innocence and infirmary, spiritual depravity and fair respite"; the ultimate opposition is shown clearly here in this public vindication of the law, and the superior assertion at the very moment of death of the nobility of a pure human spirit. *Moby-Dick* ends in darkness and desolation, for the challenge of Ahab's pride is rebuked by the physical power and the inhumanness of Nature; but *Billy Budd* ends in a brightness of escape, such as the apostle saw when he exclaimed, "O death, where is thy sting!" (135)

Before going on, one must look at the quotation from Melville's "note." Freeman was relying on the footnote which Weaver placed at the end of chapter 25, after the news account of the death of the admirable John Claggart and the depraved William Budd: "An author's note, crossed out, here appears in the original MS. It reads:—Here ends a story not unwarranted by what happens in this incongruous world of ours—innocence and infirmary, spiritual depravity and fair respite" (112). (Elsewhere I talk about the important point that the "note" applied only to an early stage of the story, not to any stages after the development of Vere.) Now, you might think that Weaver would have questioned some of his readings, and you might think that a literary Englishman would have wondered what "infirmary" had to do with "innocence" (whether as a similar or a dissimilar quality) and what "fair respite" had to do with "spiritual depravity" (although here at least an opposition is suggested by the difference between "fair" and "depravity"). What could he have thought the "note" meant? (As we saw, Hayford and Sealts transcribe the "note" this way: "Here ends a story not unwarranted by what sometimes happens in this incongruous [?] world of ours—Innocence and infamy, spiritual depravity and fair repute".)

Freeman apparently not only saw nothing in the words to perturb him but actually found in it some "ultimate opposition" which had something to do with "public vindication of the law." The "note" stirred him to write a powerful concluding tribute:

> Finished but a few months before the author's death and only lately published, *Billy Budd* shows the imaginative faculty still secure and powerful, after nearly forty years' supineness, and the not less striking security of Melville's inward peace. After what storms and secret spiritual turbulence we do not know, except by hints which it is easy to exaggerate, in his last days he re-enters an Eden-like sweetness and serenity, "with calm of mind, all passion spent", and sets his brief, appealing tragedy for witness that evil is defeat and natural goodness invincible in the affections of man. In this, the simplest of stories, told with but little of the old digressive vexatiousness, and based upon recorded incidents, Herman Melville uttered his everlasting yea, and died before a soul had been allowed to hear him. (135-36)

This eloquent passage conveys its compliments to Melville both overtly and by the casual comparison of his mood to that proclaimed by the chorus at the end of Milton's "late masterpiece," *Samson Agonistes*, "with calm of mind, all passion spent." Freeman's analysis is at some points astonishingly intuitive (especially as to the storms and secret spiritual turbulences Melville had experienced). It is also at points slightly erroneous as to fact (he apparently thought Melville had based his story on a real news report), and—very oddly—it comes to a conclusion about the invincibility of natural goodness in the affections of man which is the opposite of the conclusion Melville had once come to about the powerlessness of natural goodness to achieve a fair reputation during life or after death.

It is very hard to understand how Freeman managed to be comfortable with the words he was reading in the Constable edition. Hayford and Sealts show that the "coda" or "note" was canceled because it no longer applied to the expanded story: it worked as an interim moral for one phase of the story then was literally "unintelligible" when applied to the enlarged story. The mistranscribed version of the "coda" which Freeman read did not make *any* sense, yet he blandly reprinted the words (probably only the second time they had been printed) and used them (by some mental juggling or shifting) in justifying his comments on public vindication of the law and assertion of the nobility of a pure human spirit—the last precisely what the coda does *not* say. The fact that Freeman wrote as he did about these words (words which misrepresent Melville as appallingly as the words of the news account misrepresented Billy) reminds us that he, like Murry, was not looking closely at the words anywhere in *Billy Budd, Foretopman*.

It is not a criticism of Freeman to say that particular words hardly mattered to the British enthusiasts of the 1920s. We need to be realistic in studying how any lost literary reputation is revived, and in particular how Melville's reputation was revived, in painful slowness, between the 1880s and the early 1920s. It was revived less by literary analysis than by high-powered exclamations from high-powered literary personalities. The earnest professor Archibald MacMechan who wrote Melville a letter of praise in 1889 waited a decade to publish the first detailed argument for putting *Moby-Dick* into a high place in the canon of English and American literature. But MacMechan, writing from Dalhousie University (which would have seemed an obscure provincial place to the sophisticates at the center of literary life) did not have what we call literary clout. A mass audience pays attention when a popular novelist or a fashionable critic is quoted in the *Times* of London or the *New York Times* as having uttered the equivalent of "Wow!" In such instances, analysis is not expected, only enthusiasm; and there is no point being cynical about the process. Good often comes of such recommendations, for many readers will seize their next chance to glance at a book by the unknown writer who has so excited a literary celebrity or popular journalist.

Strange and disillusioning as this may seem, Murry, Freeman, and the other British admirers who established the reputation of *Billy Budd* on the basis of Weaver's 1924 text were not reading anywhere as near as closely as a modern literary critic is expected to read. They did not have to, writing as they were in the ecstatic glow of the rediscovery of Melville. And their success was such that as early as 1927 the novelist E. M. Forster in *Aspects of the Novel* (New York: Harcourt, Brace) took the high reputation of *Billy Budd* as a given:

> *Billy Budd* is a remote unearthly episode, but it is a song not without words, and should be read both for its own beauty and as an introduction to more difficult works. Evil is labelled and personified instead of slipping over the ocean and round the world, and Melville's mind can be observed more easily.... Melville—after the initial roughness of his realism—reaches straight back into the universal, to a blackness and sadness so transcending our own that they are undistinguishable from glory. (184)

Forster saw the story, not unreasonably, as valuable (he meant because of its brevity) for introducing new readers to Melville. British enthusiasts of the Melville Revival no longer recommended *Typee* (1846) or *Omoo* (1847) as introductions to *Moby-Dick*. Forster dreaded, with good reason, that the reader who came to Melville's first two books before reading any of his greater works would classify him as having nothing more to offer than charming reportage. Forster had a valid point, for Melville is a hard author to introduce to a new reader. *Mardi* (1849) is a grab-bag book only Melvilleans love. Not even all Melvilleans love *Pierre* and *The Confidence-Man* (1857), although there will always be a few amazed readers who finish one or another of these two so dazzled that, for at least a few hours, they prefer it to *Moby-Dick*. *White-Jacket*? *White-Jacket* has been sufficiently admired only once, in the best British reviews in 1850, yet it is a book of great power and charm, and there are passages of prose which are in the same great Melvillean voice as much of *Moby-Dick*, but late twentieth-century readers are not going to rush to read a book of a young sailor's voyage home from the Pacific in a man-of-war in the early 1840s. So most Melville readers now are introduced to him by one story or another—"Bartleby" (1853), most often, one of the world's great short stories, but worthless as an introduction to the earlier books. "Benito Cereno" (1855)? A good choice, for the great rich Melvillean style is here as it is not in "Bartleby," but teachers often are frustrated in trying to reconcile the text with their ideologies. *Billy Budd*? Probably. Forster was not far off the mark: now the first works by Melville that readers encounter are most likely to be *Moby-Dick*, "Bartleby," and *Billy Budd*—and perhaps more people now read *Billy Budd* first than read *Moby-Dick* first.

The lavish praise and instant canonization of *Billy Budd, Foretopman* by Melville's British admirers created a market for the text in America that the Constable edition could not supply, so in 1928 Weaver included it in his *Shorter Novels of Herman Melville* (New York: Horace Liveright), with a few minor alterations to the text. What Weaver wrote then, after the British critics had praised *Billy Budd*, does not seem to be by the same man who had dismissed the novel in his biography:

> In *Pierre*, Melville had hurled himself into a fury of vituperation against the world; with *Billy Budd* he would justify the ways of God to man. Among the many parallels of contrast between these two books, each is a tragedy (as was Melville's life), but in opposed sense of the term. For tragedy may be viewed not as being essentially the representation of human misery, but rather as the representation of human goodness or nobility. All of the supremest art is tragic: but the tragedy is, in Aristotle's phrase, "the representation of Eudaimonia," or the highest kind of happiness. . . . Only when worldly disaster has worked its utmost can we realize that there remains something in man's soul which is for ever beyond the grasp of the accidents of existence, with power in its own right to make life beautiful. Only through tragedy of this type could Melville affirm his everlasting yea. The final great revelation—or great illusion—of his life, he uttered in *Billy Budd*. (li)

(The "everlasting yea," of course, was a reference to Thomas Carlyle's *Sartor Resartus*, picked up, in Weaver's characteristic magpie fashion, from Freeman.)

In his critical biography *Herman Melville* (New York: Harcourt, Brace, 1929), Lewis Mumford relied on Weaver for most of his facts and seemed to echo Weaver's early unenthusiastic attitude toward *Billy Budd*. Like Freeman, Mumford quoted the "note" (what Hayford and Sealts call a "coda") as if Melville had meant it to apply to the entire manuscript, not merely to the stage before he had elaborated the characterization of Vere:

> Billy Budd is the story of three men in the British Navy: it is also the story of the world, the spirit, and the devil. Melville left a note, crossed out in the original manuscript, "here ends a story not unwarranted by what happens in this incongruous world of ours—innocence and infirmity, spiritual depravity and fair respite." The meaning is so obvious that one shrinks from underlining it. Good and evil exist in the nature of things, each forever itself, each doomed to war with the other. In the working out of human institutions, evil has a place as well as the good: Vere is contemptuous of Claggart, but cannot do without him: he loves Budd as a son and must condemn him to the noose: justice dictates an act abhorrent to his nature, and only his inner magnanimity keeps it from being revolting. These are the fundamental ambiguities of life: so long as evil exists, the agents that intercept it will also be evil, whilst we accept the world's conditions: those universal articles of war on which our civilizations rest. Rascality may be punished; but beauty and innocence will suffer in that process far more. There is no comfort, in this perpetual Calvary, to find a thief nailed on either side of the Cross. Melville had been harried by these paradoxes in Pierre. At last he was reconciled. He accepted the situation as a tragic necessity; and to meet that tragedy bravely was to find peace, the ultimate peace of resignation, even in an incongruous world. (356-57)

The quotation was taken not from the 1924 text but from Weaver's 1928 edition (the first American edition). Without realizing it, apparently, Mumford was quoting a new reading in the "coda"— "infirmity" instead of "infirmary." That was still a distance from what Melville wrote, "infamy." The whole passage is fascinating, not least because it asserts that the meaning is too "obvious" to emphasize when in fact it is incomprehensible in the form he quotes it (not only with "infirmity" instead of "infamy," but also with "fair respite" instead of "fair repute"); furthermore, it incorporates into the ringing conclusion a word ("incongruous") which may or may not be an accurate transcription of what Melville wrote at that point in the manuscript.

E. L. Grant Watson, the British naturalist and literary man, published in 1930 in the *New England Quarterly* a reading of *Pierre* which for decades stood as the most sensitive tribute to that book. He followed it in the same journal with a 1933 article on *Billy Budd* as "Melville's Testament of Acceptance"—with "testament" carrying the sense of last will but also the scriptural sense, for he saw the work as Melville's "gospel story" (321). Melville himself, Watson said, in *Billy Budd* is "no longer a rebel" (322), nor is Billy. Rather, the "supreme quality of acceptance" marks Billy, and Captain Vere as well (323). Drawing some phraseology from the essay Melville wrote in 1850 on Hawthorne's *Mosses from an Old Manse*, Watson stressed the provocative, haunting qualities of the work:

> There are darker hints: those deep, far-away things in Vere, those occasional flashings-forth of intuition—short, quick probings to the very axis of reality. Though the book be read many times, the student may still remain baffled by Melville's significant arrangement of images. The story is so solidly filled out as to suggest dimensions in all directions. As soon as the mind fastens upon one subject, others flash into being. (324)

Watson related these observations to Melville's own psychological probings in *Pierre*, where Melville had "peered as deep as any into the origins of sensuality, and in conscious understanding he was the equal of any modern psychologist; in poetic divination he has the advantage of most." Melville knew what he was doing:

> In this book of his old age, the images which he chose for the presentation of his final wisdom, move between the antinomies of love and hate, of innocence and malice. From behind—from far behind the main pageant of the story—there seem to fall suggestive shadows of primal, sexual simplicities. In so conscious a symbolist as Melville, it would be surprising if there should be no meaning or half-meaning in the spilling of Billy's soup towards the homosexually-disposed Claggart, in the impotence of Billy's speech in the presence of his accuser, in his swift and deadly answer, or the likening of Claggart's limp, dead body to that of a snake. (324-25)

Watson looked in "this final book" for a "further, deeper wisdom" (325) than in *Pierre* or *Clarel*, and not a wisdom that gives itself away:

> In this short history of the impressment and hanging of a handsome sailor-boy, are to be discovered problems almost as profound as those which puzzle us in the pages of the Gospels. *Billy Budd* is a book to be read many times, for at each reading it will light up, as do the greater experiences of life, a beyond leading always into the unknown. (327)

Celebrating, like Murry, rather than closely analyzing, Watson confirmed the reputation of *Billy Budd* as a major late work. His own reputation was so deservedly high after his dazzling reading of *Pierre* that he *could* help effect that confirmation in this country, where no men and women of letters (with the exception of Mumford) came forward to ratify the canonization.

In the United States through the 1920s there were few outspoken champions of Melville among the major writers, in contrast to England, where one famous writer after another fell under Melville's spell. Many American writers missed almost all the furor about Melville in England and the mild stir about him in the United States: in the 1920s to think of yourself as a good American writer often meant living in Paris or somewhere else on the Continent and coming home as little as possible. Faulkner in the late 1920s said that *Moby-Dick* was the book he most wished he had written. Hemingway by the early 1930s had heard about *Moby-Dick* enough to scoff at it, perhaps without having read it. F. Scott Fitzgerald did not include Melville in the "College for One" he set up for Sheilah Graham in the late 1930s. In the late 1930s Edith Wharton mentioned hearing disparagement of Melville in her post–Civil War childhood, but she knew that he was by blood closely connected with the finest Dutch families of New York. She did not say so, but she probably knew that he was a cousin of her dear friend Walter Berry. (As children Berry and his sister had vacationed with Melville's mother and his sister Augusta at Gansevoort, New York, in the early 1860s. Indeed, since Augusta was a faithful correspondent with Berry's mother, he may very well have had some of Augusta's letters in his great library when Wharton knew him in Paris.) Yet while American novelists had nothing to do, really, with rediscovering Melville, some of them at least picked up some reverberations of the English enthusiasm. In 1957 an alert student at the University of Virginia asked Faulkner if his character Thomas Sutpen were like Claggart in *Billy Budd* or Iago in *Othello*, and Faulkner's reply as given in *Faulkner in the University* does not make it clear whether he had read Melville's story or not. Perhaps he hadn't—perhaps like many other people he regarded Melville as a man of one book. It was primarily through British influence that Melville by 1940 or so had come to be thought of, often enough, as the writer of *Moby-Dick* and *Billy Budd*—surely an astonishing development to Frank Jewett Mather, Jr., who had loved Melville for half a century and first sampled the pages of *Billy Budd* in 1906 or earlier.

This case history of the instant canonization of *Billy Budd, Foretopman* is anything but simple, it seems to me. The language of the first critics of the novel suggests that much more was involved than consolidation of political or sexual power over the canon. Knowledge of *Moby-Dick* had stirred up intense aesthetic, philosophical, and psychological (as well as sexual and spiritual) impulses in many of the brightest and most earnest literary people in England, of all generations, and they saw *Billy Budd, Foretopman* as a treasure from the grave. Political motivations, if present, are not obvious. Certainly no English writer gloated chauvinistically at getting the jump on Americans by being first to recognize a great American writer (this although over the last several decades many Britishers had deplored the failure of Americans to recognize the greatness of Melville—and Whitman and Thoreau). If there is a politico-cultural agenda in these discoverers of *Billy Budd, Foretopman*, locating it will require strenuous delving into the lives of Murry, Freeman, Forster, and others.

Modern theorists eager to charge that the exaltation of Melville's final novel was the product of male sexism will encounter complexities from the start. We know that many of Melville's early admirers in England were homosexual men, and we know that there were female admirers of Melville in England through the end of the nineteenth century and into the Revival; indeed, by an accident of timing Viola Meynell with her introduction to the Oxford edition of *Moby-Dick* in 1920 helped precipitate the final phase of the Revival. We know that some of the admirers of Melville in the London of the early 1920s were bisexual or homosexual men and women. (I have told the story in the "Historical Note" to the Northwestern-Newberry edition of *Moby-Dick*.) Before anyone can claim there was a hidden sexual agenda in the canonizing of *Billy Budd, Foretopman*, much research needs to be done. The researcher might discover that women (whatever their sexuality) participated in the reception of *Billy Budd, Foretopman*. If women did, my bet (based on what Virginia Woolf and others were saying about Melville) is that their voices will be all but indistinguishable from the voices of male reviewers (of any sexual orientation).

Aside from any political and sexual aspects, this history supports the assertion I made at the outset—that there is not necessarily a close relationship between the coherence of a work and the value that becomes attached to it. Psychologically alert rhetoricians might want to use *Billy Budd, Foretopman* in experiments in reading, to see, for instance, whether their students will invariably expound upon the functions of the "preface." (Someone reading *Billy Budd, Sailor* in the light of Hayford and Sealts's evidence that even their edition is not a perfectly formed and completely finished work of art might find some value in the evidence that the book—even when properly transcribed—is in parts incoherent—might, as students of Melville's mind, find value even in sad evidence of the deterioration of his powers and of what they might see as his intermittent mustering of the powers remaining to him.) To the baffling question of how the critics of the Revival were able to exalt a work even while quoting passages which did not make sense, a facile answer would be that the Melville enthusiasts were so grateful for something they could call a late masterpiece—for a Melville work first published in their own time—that they simply did not pause to read the passages they were quoting. A more satisfying answer would draw upon the work of cognitive psychologists on the brain's built-in tendency to make sense of whatever it tries to focus on. Our assumption that all texts are coherent suggests that the range of misuses of a literary work is wider than the adaptive use (or "misuse") that Barbara Herrnstein Smith points to in her 1983 article or in *Contingencies of Value* (1988).

Anyone who reflects on the situation I have described will find further complications and further topics to be explored. One question immediately arises: should we expect a niche in the hall of canonical literature to be held for a "text" no matter how much one text differs from another going by the same name or by a close variant of that name? Some readers in the 1960s felt bereft when the familiar nonprefatory "preface" was not in *Billy Budd, Sailor*, but no one declared that *Billy Budd, Sailor* had to undergo a whole new canonization process if it were to take the niche already granted to *Billy Budd, Foretopman*. *Billy Budd*, apparently, was canonized—not just *Billy Budd, Foretopman*.

# Chapter Six

## Close-Reading a Flawed Text

AMERICAN (AND CANADIAN) PROFESSORS HAD NO ROLE AT ALL IN ES-
tablishing a high place for *Billy Budd* in the body of Melville's
writings, but their first comments on the story, toward the end of
the 1930s and early 1940s, showed that they had assimilated what
the earlier British admirers had written. When Carl Van Doren in
1940 called *Billy Budd* a story in which Melville came to full
mastery of himself, his imagination, and his material (*The American Novel, 1789-1939*), he was confirming the British writers. By
1940 in his article on Melville's "metaphysics of evil" R. E. Watters
could loftily hold up the power of love in *Billy Budd* as a pattern
man imprints on the blackness of the cosmos. It became customary
for American writers to deck their discussions of the story with
solemn comparisons to Sophocles and Shakespeare (Willard
Thorp, 1941); to Milton in *Paradise Regained* (Edward Weeks,
1941); *The Tempest* (W. E. Sedgwick, 1944). Scholarship on *Billy
Budd* began with Charles Roberts Anderson's 1940 essay in *American Literature*, which suggested that the origin of *Billy Budd* was
an article on the *Somers* mutiny of 1842 published in 1888. (Hayford and Sealts have shown that although the mutiny was indeed
on Melville's mind in his late years, he seems not to have been
focusing on it during the first years of his work on the story, but
instead to have been reminded of it again fairly late during the
course of the writing.) Detailed academic *criticism*, what we think
of as "close reading" of the text, began with great appropriateness,
in the quintessentially New Critical journal, *The Explicator* (December 1943). There T. T. E. observed that in chapter 6 the narrator

speaks admiringly of Vere's disinterested mental processes, but later makes Vere's arguments at the trial hinge on the "practical consequences" if Billy is not hanged at once. T. T. E. asked: "Are we to regard this disparity as an oversight or as one of the essential ambiguities in the story? Does it perhaps point the way to regarding the novel as rather more concerned with social repercussions and less concerned with personal ethics than is customary? In this respect the 'Preface' deserves especial note" (Item Q14). This first piece of academic criticism demonstrates the problematic nature of the characterization of Vere, evident when anyone pays close attention to the words in any text, not just the Weaver text; and it also demonstrates the great good sense of academic criticism, where a "Preface" ought to be given special attention for the clues it offers for reading the rest of the work. (T. T. E. was an innocent victim of a bad text, but he or she was also an excellent reader.)

Predictably, *The Explicator* received a reply to T. T. E., and the academic arguments over *Billy Budd* were launched. Notice, however, that the arguments were not over the value, which the British admirers had established—they were merely over points of interpretation. And the arguments, all centering on the character of Captain Vere, gained momentum during the 1950s as the teaching of American literature at the college and university level became customary—teaching which (like the teaching of British and Continental literature) had been transformed in the late 1940s under the influence of the New Criticism (best instilled by Cleanth Brooks and Robert Penn Warren in their popular textbooks). In the 1950s it became fashionable to think of each work (each poem, each story, each novel—to the gradual decline of interest in nonfictional prose) as wholly discrete, containing its own unique structure which the reader could perceive by paying very close attention to "the work itself," in whatever text the reader held. This critical approach encouraged total confidence that the text in hand was absolutely complete and perfect—ready for interpretation. Whatever their limitations, the critics who approached *Billy Budd* with such confidence during this decade were determined to fit minor details of the text into their demonstrations of the larger meanings.

A number of close-reading critics through the 1950s expressed uneasiness about the notion that *Billy Budd* was Melville's "everlasting yea" (Freeman's term) or Melville's "testament of acceptance" (Watson's term, adapted from Murry, and the term that came to stand for any reading that saw the story as marking a drastic turn away from defiance toward submission). Following a suggestion by Gay Wilson Allen that the story should be read ironically, Joseph Schiffman (in the May 1950 *American Literature*) wrote not primarily about *Billy Budd* but (for the first time) about criticism on *Billy Budd*: "Melville's Final Stage, Irony: A Re-Examination of *Billy Budd* Criticism." Like the reviewers of the 1920s, Schiffman resorted to exclamation rather than analysis:

> At heart a kind man, Vere, strange to say, makes possible the depraved Claggart's wish—the destruction of Billy. "God bless Captain Vere!" Is this not piercing irony? As innocent Billy utters these words, does not the reader gag? The injustice of Billy's hanging is heightened by his ironic blessing of the ironic Vere. (133)

In this reading, irony (that indispensable word of the New Critics) was Melville's new weapon of social and political protest, his last weapon "in his lifelong fight against injustice" (133). At the end of the decade (in the June 1959 *Modern Language Quarterly*) Phil Withim frankly turned Watson's title back on him with his essay *"Billy Budd*: Testament of Resistance." Calmer than Schiffman, Withim carried forward the same argument. His assumption about the wholeness of a work of art was purely New Critical: "This paper . . . accepts the point of view that *Billy Budd* was written in a basically ironic style; it will attempt to establish a thesis in harmony with all of the parts of the story and to demonstrate that the 'testament of acceptance' theory is essentially self-contradictory" (115-16). Naturally, Withim found that the preface (the authenticity of which was still unchallenged) "helps to make clear the direction of the book" (121), but the moral Withim found in it was that tyranny could be successfully resisted, not that the times were so dangerous that authority had to assert itself with unusual force and promptness. Demanding that we read Melville's praise of Vere as sarcasm, Withim appealed for proof to the pages that Melville devotes to the heroic Nelson:

> Nelson, of course, dies a soldier's death, while Vere dies drugged and ashore before ever reaching fame. Nelson is a fighter in direct contact with the enemy; but Vere, in the encounter described in

> *Billy Budd*, does not have an opportunity to catch the opposing ship. Vere is frequently used for diplomatic missions, the very opposite of a captain's usual job; Vere, says Melville, though a man of "sturdy qualities was without brilliant ones." Nelson is asked to take command of a ship recently involved in the Great Mutiny, for "it was thought that an officer like Nelson was the one, *not indeed to terrorize the crew into base subjection*, but to win them, by force of his mere presence back to an allegiance if not as enthusiastic as his own, yet as true." . . . Vere, in a similar situation, hangs Billy, "thinking perhaps that under existing circumstances in the navy the consequence of violating discipline should be made to speak for itself." (117-18)

In Withim's view the implied comparison was distinctly unfavorable to Vere. As a New Critic, Withim did not think of going to the manuscript for evidence about the status of the Nelson chapter, but in fact he could have found much stronger arguments had he done so. Those arguments are discussed below.

At the end of the 1950s, then, interpretation was polarized—Vere was good and Melville liked him (as any decent person would), Vere was bad and Melville despised him (as any decent person would). Despite all the debate, no one suggested that *Billy Budd* was overrated or meaningless. It had been hyped into the canon, or elected by acclamation, but it was staying there securely. It managed to do so for any number of reasons. Melville's reputation grew through the 1950s, as *The Confidence-Man* and *Pierre* gained readers, and the status of *Billy Budd* as great posthumous novel was assured. As I suggested at the outset, its brevity was a factor both in its easy entrance into the canon and in its remaining there: short final masterpieces (and really any important short works) are flexibly *usable* in the classroom. Certainly *Billy Budd* was just the right size for a New Critical assignment: "Do a *Searching* Explication of *Billy Budd*." It was not available separately in the United States (the first separate publication in English had appeared in London in 1946, following separate publication in French, German, and Italian translations), but it was conveniently available in paperback editions of Melville stories, in classroom anthologies, and even in a casebook (1961) prepared by William T. Stafford (and revised in 1968). (The vogue at this time for collections of text plus criticism is a significant academic phenomenon; like other editors, Stafford specified that one use of his collection would be as a source book in composition courses, particularly in new colleges where the library holdings were limited.) And while no one agreed completely with anyone else about what it meant, *Billy Budd* indisputably held power to move its readers, the teasing, upsetting, tormenting, and even outraging power found only in more ambiguous-seeming works of literature. Perhaps never before or since the 1950s has literary ambiguity (like "irony" an essential word in the New Critical vocabulary) been so unabashedly valued. Whether in a given chapter the ambiguity was authorially contrived or merely inadvertent no one thought of trying to distinguish—no one except a pair of young professors whose achievement is the subject of the chapter after next.

*Chapter Seven*

---

# Textual Curiosity in the New Critical 1950s

---

IN THE FOLLOWING PARAGRAPHS, AS I DEAL WITH *BILLY BUDD*, UN-known in early 1924, yet a standard work of American literature a quarter century later, I will be talking about the teaching of American literature in American colleges and universities as if it began in the late 1940s. In many colleges it did begin then, although some others had offered courses in American literature years or even decades before. (The attitude that American literature was too recent and too provincial to be taught in colleges survived in many English departments into the early 1960s, and even beyond. Ask an older professor how inferior one's classmates and some professors of English literature tried to make anyone feel for taking a course in American literature.) Textbooks used in such courses before the 1940s very seldom included selections from Melville, whose renown in England in the 1920s took a long time to filter into the consciousness of American professors and even longer to reach American grade school or high schools (if you don't count a short whaling excerpt from *Moby-Dick* in *Harper's Fifth Reader*, 1889). (Irving, the New England poets, Emerson, Hawthorne, and other American writers entered grade school and high school curricula *first* then were inducted into advanced courses as soon as colleges and universities began to teach American literature.) The acceptance of Melville into the canon quickly followed the securing of American literature in the typical curriculum, and both came, as you would expect, in boom times, when new courses (with some new writers) can be introduced without bloodletting in departmental committees. The boom was the post–World War II expansion in college enrollment and the consequent expansion of old schools and the creation of new ones at all levels (including the astonishing proliferation of two-year colleges).

As luck had it the expansion of colleges and the patriotic inclusion of courses in American literature coincided with the triumph of the new approach to teaching literature and writing about literature mentioned above. This approach—the New Criticism—did not emphasize archival study and indeed discouraged the reader from drawing on any evidence other than that of the words of the printed text which he or she held in hand. The new libraries could not overnight become equivalents of the established research institutions, and under the dominant approach to literature they did not *have* to; appropriately, the great number of critical (not scholarly) journals founded in the 1950s and 1960s for the most part published "readings" written on the basis of "the text" rather than on biographical, textual, or historical evidence. (See two 1987 accounts, Kermit Vanderbilt's *American Literature and the Academy* and Gerald Graff's *Professing Literature: An Institutional History*.)

Through the 1950s and 1960s and on to the present most college professors have assigned texts without regard to the compositional and publishing history of those texts and have taught them as if one could always teach a book from "the text itself" without regard to "external" or "extrinsic" evidence—the sort of evidence which might have undercut the sanctity of "the text itself." They regularly looked for patterns in a text by which the whole text could be understood—without paying attention to evidence that, for instance, in *The Red Badge of Courage* the twelfth chapter and parts of other chapters had been removed in 1895, before publication: the "whole" from which the function of the parts was being deduced was *not* in fact the "whole" that the author had written and had tried for many months to get published. Before the early 1950s no one taught Stephen Crane's *Maggie: A Girl of the Streets* in any form other than the severely expurgated version published in 1896, so any comments that teachers (and critics) made on overall image or thematic patterns, on foreshadowing (especially on foreshadowing through a pattern of overlapping characterizations), and anything else having to do with the unity or disunity of the "whole" text, was said about the text from which the prostitute's final encounter with a gross fat man (an encounter which immediately preceded her death) had been totally excised. Theodore Dreiser's *Sister Carrie* was widely taught as a classic text of American naturalism, but until 1981 no one was able to teach a text that contained what Dreiser had actually written. There are many such examples, disproportionally huddled in the realistic and naturalistic periods, when the most daring representatives of the new literary movements were extremely likely to face some sort of censorship in their attempts to get their works into print (so that many writers had to settle for getting *most* of a work into print).

Despite their New Critical indoctrination (which might have predisposed them to disregard *any* new textual and biographical evidence), academic critics have often been able to adjust rapidly and reasonably to such new evidence. As soon as scholars began pointing out, in the 1950s, that the original version of *Maggie* (1893) was not only an extremely rare and breathtakingly pricy little paperback but also contained a text much superior to the expurgated Appleton text of 1896, almost everybody, pretty fast, stopped citing the 1896 edition. This was made easy because several new editions (including three photographic facsimiles) of the 1893 *Maggie* were published to take advantage of the new demand for the fuller, uncensored text. Therefore just a few years after the poet John Berryman's brilliant book on Crane was published, critics could look back and wish they could know what he would have written had he read the unexpurgated *Maggie*. Critics have responded similarly to the Dreiser *Sister Carrie*, for the most part, although there have been some vehement arguments for continuing to read what we had all always read, even though it was much farther from what the author wrote than the new (i.e., original), much longer text. The new reconstructed *The Red Badge of Courage*, unlike the *Maggie*, has not prevailed over the Appleton edition (1895). I suspect it was easy for professors to adjust to the new (i.e., original) *Maggie* because few of them had been teaching it from the 1896 text and very few of them had written on it. Furthermore, it was out of print and cost no royalties to reproduce, although a copy of the original would cost thousands of dollars. By contrast, the reconstructed *Red Badge* was copyrighted; worse, since *every* Crane critic had a vested interest in the 1895 Appleton text, not every critic could take a fully objective view of the evidence and learn from it.

In the 1950s, and up until 1962, while such new textual information about several famous American literary works was gradually emerging, teachers of *Billy Budd* dealt with a work which began with a "Preface" Melville did not write as a preface; which contained the discarded "Lawyers, Experts, Clergy" passage; and which contained many dozens of words which were misreadings of the words Melville wrote. Editions available for classroom use were most often reprints of Weaver's 1928 text, but the situation had been complicated by Harvard's publishing in hardback in 1948 a new edition edited by F. Barron Freeman, who had worked with the manuscript, which had been deposited in the Houghton Library at Harvard by Melville's granddaughter, Eleanor Metcalf. Freeman's text was meant to replace Weaver's. The wise transcriber of a manuscript always rejects help in the early stages, saying, in effect, "Don't tell me. Let me make it out for myself." Freeman did not make a fresh transcription of the manuscript with no prompting on the hard spots but instead simply marked his corrections in a copy of Weaver's text, with the predictable result that (probably quite unconsciously) he was guided by his "pony" and preserved many of its verbal errors, and because he failed to rethink all the textual evidence he followed Weaver in gross features such as the inclusion of the preface which was not a preface. Various Melville scholars looked at the manuscript in the late 1940s and early 1950s, Leon Howard long enough to conclude, rightly, that the whole work had grown out of Melville's headnote to the ballad of "Billy in the Darbies." Such scholars pointed out errors in Weaver and Freeman, so that Harvard University Press in 1951 "temporarily" withdrew the Freeman text from sale and had one of its editors, Elizabeth Treeman, check Freeman's text against the manuscript. In 1952 she entered her corrections in a copy of *Billy Budd* that was later used in preparing the text of a standard anthology, *The American Tradition in Literature*. The next year Harvard issued her pamphlet, *Corrigenda*, and again listed the Freeman text as in print and kept it in print five more years (with the intention that the pamphlet would accompany each copy sold). Editors of other anthologies made an effort to incorporate some of Treeman's corrections, and anthology-makers began referring to

their using, or their having consulted, the "Freeman-Treeman edition," something that never existed. The details are unimportant:
the point is that in the 1950s some editors (or "introducers") of
classroom texts of *Billy Budd*, including the texts in best-selling
anthologies, tried to be responsible, within the limits of the information readily at hand. Everyone knew that some Melville experts
were dissatisfied with the text, but no one said that the textual
situation of *Billy Budd* was comparable to that of *Maggie*, for
instance, or that of *The Red Badge of Courage* (about which textual information also began to become available in the 1950s).

*Chapter Eight*

---

# The Hayford-Sealts Edition (1962)

---

IN THE LATE 1950S AND EARLY 1960S TWO AMERICAN LITERATURE PRO-
fessors, Harrison Hayford of Northwestern University and Merton
M. Sealts, Jr., then of Lawrence College, later of the University of
Wisconsin at Madison, spent their summers together in the
Houghton Library transcribing and analyzing the manuscript of
*Billy Budd*. Their edition was published by the University of Chicago Press in 1962, seventy-one years after Melville's death. It included a clear reading text based upon their fresh study of the
manuscript. In the reading text they left out what Melville had left
out and put in what he had put in, and tidied up some punctuation and a few forms of words where they felt they had to, but not
to the point of disguising the unfinished nature of the work. (The
one complication in the way of their leaving out what Melville left
out and putting in what he put in is the Nelson chapter, discussed
below. There Melville's own indecisiveness prevents any editorial
decision from being wholly satisfactory.) They also published a
genetic text, one showing (through symbols and editorial comments) the growth of each sentence as far as the surviving evidence
allowed and the use and reuse of the individual leaves (and parts
of leaves) of the manuscript.

Hayford and Sealts showed that Freeman had misunderstood
the course of the growth of the manuscript and had come to the
quite erroneous conclusion that Melville had first written a short
story, "Baby Budd, Sailor," out of which he had then composed
the longer story. This had some importance for criticism, since
writers of essays on *Billy Budd* had naturally accepted Freeman's

claims. Hayford and Sealts concluded that no such short story ever existed: "At no stage of the composition of *Billy Budd* did Melville have a version constituting, corresponding to, or even approximating the text Freeman mistakenly presented under the title 'Baby Budd, Sailor'" (17). Much more important, the Hayford-Sealts edition was the first to recover all the words of the manuscript (the only word they were not sure of ["incongruous"?] was not in the final manuscript, but in the already discussed "coda," which Melville had canceled) and to work out the priority of inscription of the leaves and thereby to establish the order in which the story grew. It was also "the first to reject the supposed 'Preface,' to exclude the 'Lawyers, Experts, Clergy' episode from the final text, and to use the author's own final title" (20).

The reception of the Hayford-Sealts *Billy Budd, Sailor* falls somewhere in the middle range of cases where teachers have had to adjust to drastically unfamiliar texts, nearer the triumph of the unexpurgated *Maggie* than the reconstructed *Red Badge*, yet widely ignored for many years and in some quarters the subject of vehement criticism, so that more than a decade passed before the Chicago text became anything like standard. Many professors (whether in their role as classroom teacher or anthology editor) simply did not think a different text of a little novel could make much difference. As Bruce Harkness pointed out at this time in an immediately controversial essay on "Bibliography and the Novelistic Fallacy" (*Studies in Bibliography* 12 [1959]) most teachers were already so indoctrinated by the New Criticism that they could not take seriously the idea that novels might have textual problems worth attending to: mistakes might matter in Elizabethan drama and would probably always matter in poetry, but mistakes here and there would be undetectable in the mass of words in a novel.

Most reviewers for academic journals, a decade and more into the era of the New Criticism, were unable to follow Hayford and Sealts's analysis of the growth of the manuscript and were unwilling to consider giving up their starting point in classroom discussions of the book, the familiar "Preface." The managing editor of *Modern Fiction Studies*, William T. Stafford, in an issue of that journal devoted to Herman Melville (vol. 8, Autumn 1962), carefully described Hayford and Sealts's work in "The New *Billy Budd* and the Novelistic Fallacy: An Essay-Review," the title of which showed that he had read Harkness and was well-prepared to think about the interpretive significance of textual problems in the novel. Stafford was unusual in his openness to the evidence, particularly since he saw that he would have to change the text in his casebook on *Billy Budd* if it were ever reprinted. In the most influential academic journal in the field, *American Literature* (vol. 36, March 1964), Lawrance Thompson denounced the "unacceptable attempt to throw out the 'Preface'" (79) and said wishfully (78), "Perhaps Melville put the so-called 'Preface' in a separate folder because he wanted to use it, eventually, as a 'Preface.' No other 'Preface' for *Billy Budd* has been found." The harshest criticism from the early reviews of the Chicago edition through to the present has focused on the fact that Hayford and Sealts did not print as "Preface" the words which everyone who knew the book had always encountered first every time he or she started to read the book. Those who felt as if they had been robbed of familiar passages did not particularly care whether or not Melville himself had rejected the passages, on second or third or later thought. What mattered to them was that as far as they were concerned *Billy Budd* had always come with a "Preface" and always should come with a "Preface."

This may seem a strange attitude for people to take who ought to be interested in what the author wanted, but it is in actuality a very common attitude. What we are dealing with is a widespread notion that the form of a text which is first published or else the form of a text which becomes well known must be taken as the "received text," the text on which criticism is to be lavished. It is always convenient when a critic understands his own assumptions about literature so thoroughly that he can state them clearly, as Milton R. Stern does in *Billy Budd, Sailor* (Indianapolis: Bobbs Merrill, 1975), an "edition" based on the Hayford-Sealts Genetic Text:

> *Billy Budd* has long been an established work in the Melville canon. Readers, critics, teachers, students are familiar with the leaves that used to be the "Preface." That portion has become a part of *Billy Budd* whether Melville intended them to be or not. (153)

Hayford and Sealts underestimated the strength of this feeling of being robbed which Stern manifests. In this non-intentionalist view, the author is not thought to incorporate his intentionality and meaning in what he writes. What confers authority is familiarity. (For a similar demand for the familiar "Preface" see also Thomas J. Scorza, *In the Time before Steamships* [DeKalb: Northern Illinois University Press, 1979], 183-95.)

Reviews which lamented the loss of the supposed "Preface" gave teachers an excuse to avoid using the Chicago text, but some of the most compelling reasons for avoiding it were financial. To teach *Billy Budd, Sailor* in 1963 meant assigning the Chicago Phoenix paperback, since the text was not yet available in a standard anthology, and then as now teachers feel pressured to assign as few textbooks as they can manage with; many were willing to make do with an earlier text of *Billy Budd, Foretopman* already available in a bargain-priced standard American literature anthology. Some teachers rationalized that they could get better bargains for their students by assigning one of several paperback selections of Melville which contained not just *Billy Budd, Foretopman* but also other of Melville's stories. Some teachers were simply tired of adjusting to adjustments in the text of *Billy Budd* every decade. In one or two instances editors and publishers had already gone to some lengths to get a reliable text and felt imposed upon when it seemed they had to go to new and still greater lengths—resetting the entire text of the story and paying royalties for it. The reviews gave all anthology-makers an excuse to avoid the text for which they would have to pay royalty to the University of Chicago (a fact of academic life is that superior texts are sometimes avoided because paying for them would eat into profits).

Hayford and Sealts pretty clearly counted on readers' working through the Genetic Text and (knowing better than anybody else how very much essential evidence was printed *only* in the Genetic Text) they apparently did not adequately realize that many readers would want to settle for only a *little* more information than the University of Chicago Press's Phoenix paperback offered, and would fiercely want that particular information there, at hand, not in the more expensive hardback. Perhaps Hayford and Sealts would agree now that they made a strategic mistake in not retaining at least their own transcription of the "1797" passage and the "experts" passage in the apparatus of the paperback edition, along with an explanation of just where the two passages had stood (when they were part of the manuscript) and how the manuscript had changed after each of the two passages had been removed. Users of the text—teachers, in particular—would have been left with all the paragraphs they had been accustomed to thinking of as the comprising the story (I can't say "all the words," because teachers were used to dozens of words and word forms which were Weaver's misreadings and which were corrected in the Chicago text), along with a rationale for explaining away their absence. (Of course, the question immediately arises: how can one include discarded portions in *reprintings* of the Chicago text? This situation has no simple solution.)

Although by 1970 or so probably a majority of critics were citing the Chicago text in their quotations from *Billy Budd*, they were extremely slow to realize that they just could not responsibly say certain things about *Billy Budd* anymore, after the Hayford-Sealts analysis of the manuscript had been published. For instance, Hayford and Sealts showed that Melville tended to write out his philosophical reflections first, then, later, to invent characters to embody some of the conflicts or to express some of the feelings:

> A final and major point is that in making the revision [involving the surgeon's attitude toward Captain Vere] Melville was doing what he had consistently done in the whole course of composition: he was *dramatizing* the situation (and its implications) which he had previously *reported*. The point may be served by a quotation from Charles Olson (1948), who preferred Freeman's composite "Baby Budd" to the supposedly later *Billy Budd*, as more dramatic. In expanding the story, Olson declared, Melville "worked over and over as though the hand that wrote was Hawthorne's, with his essayism, his hints, the veil of his syntax, until the celerity of the short story was run out, the force of the juxtapositions interrupted, and the secret of Melville as artist, the presentation of ambiguity by the event direct, was lost in the Salem manner." Actually, as we have shown, *Billy Budd* developed in almost the opposite way, from exposition into dramatization. (35-36)

One might think that after Hayford and Sealts had demonstrated the way *Billy Budd* developed critics would work that information into their analyses, but that did not happen. More than once critics ignored their evidence altogether. In 1973, for example, a writer in a respectable journal argued that Melville related incidents in his story then wrapped them in a great deal of authorial analysis—the opposite of the way Melville really worked.

Notice an interesting oddity in the example of a critic from 1973. Merely to say anything about the order of Melville's writing, his moving from analysis to incident or from incident to analysis, is to appeal to biographical evidence, against the New Critical practice. In this particular case, it is to do so without doing biographical research for oneself and (worse) without consulting or understanding the biographical (textual) work two scholars had already published. If one is going to appeal to Melville's biography, it behooves one to get biography right: otherwise, biography may be used to slight or even slur the writer (as in arguing patronizingly that Melville had the right dramatic impulse but smothered it with dull reflective passages), instead of using it to show something of genuine biographical interest (whether or not of interest for interpretation). Let me try a line of speculation just for an example (don't hold me to the position I take). For the sake of focusing the argument, one could deduce from Hayford and Sealts's information that Melville did not have an imagination primarily dramatic. That is, while William Shakespeare and Charles Dickens may have been writers whose minds were thronged with characters, vivid, absolutely individual, recognizable from afar, unforgettable, Melville might have been quite another sort of writer, one who (as he wrote of himself in his journal on 9 December 1849, in Cologne) was "a pondering man," a sort of writer who brooded first on ideas or issues that concerned him then only slowly, belatedly, began to create characters to embody some of those ideas or issues. This may not be a claim that appeals to every teacher and student, but it is at least nearer the truth than the allegation that Melville had another sort of imagination in which spontaneous dramatic scenes were overwhelmed by belated meditative passages. If we are going to make biographical judgments, in short, we might as well make them on the basic of biographical evidence, when it exists. But the sad fact is that the Hayford-Sealts labors have not made much difference to criticism.

If a teacher disregards the evidence that Hayford and Sealts assembled and analyzed and tells his or her students that *Billy Budd, Sailor* contains scenes which had been wonderfully "dramatic," full of action and dialogue, before the tedious old author smothered the drama with pages of belated, maundering commentary, is any harm done? The question is what one can say and still be intellectually responsible. Very few critics writing on *Billy Budd* since 1962 have based any of their arguments on the Genetic Text as well as the Reading Text. In not using this evidence they have often proceeded with analyses which were simply not worth doing, wrong from the start; but quite often, also, they have ignored evidence that could have clarified and greatly strengthened their arguments. The Hayford-Sealts text is now the one most commonly taught, but no critic has made good use of the full range of their evidence. The critic who made the best (though brief) start at it was Mary Everett Burton Fussell in *Studies in Romanticism* (Winter 1976). Fussell's conclusions are highly debatable, and her use of the Genetic Text is flawed (she did not take time to learn what the symbols meant), but she did the main thing right—she started using the Genetic Text to gain a sense of Melville's process of composition. Hayford and Sealts had laid out the evidence invitingly, but she was the first (and so far the last) to ask such an obvious question as this: "what significant synapses took place in Melville's mind as he flipped the pages of old poem holographs whose reverse sides he used in composing *Billy Budd?*" (46). That sort of study cries out to be made, even today, after I have made the chapter-by-chapter reading in this book.

In his essay in *A Companion to Melville Studies* (1986) Sealts made his first lengthy comments upon *Billy Budd, Sailor* since the publication of the Chicago edition. This essay drew on a lecture he gave in 1983 to a seminar for lawyers presented by the Wisconsin Humanities Committee. The greatest interest of Sealts's paper lies in his retrospective look at the hope he and Hayford had cherished for the product of their labors over the text:

> In 1962, when the Chicago edition of *Billy Budd, Sailor*, appeared, its two editors expressed the hope "that a comprehensive scholarly edition of the work will narrow the ground of disagreement and widen that of understanding" (p. v). What they wrote still remains a hope unfulfilled, however, for advances in literary scholarship do not necessarily produce corresponding advances in literary criticism. The critical reassessments of the 1950s, signalized by new readings not only of Melville but of literature gen-

erally, were relatively quiet preludes to the social and political upheavals on college and university campuses during the Vietnam years. Like their anti-war students, some academic professionals displayed little interest in the findings of textual scholarship, for those were times when imaginative literature—if it was to be read at all—either had to be politically "relevant" or made to seem so. (422)

After surveying attempts by critics to demonstrate the relevance of *Billy Budd, Sailor* to their various hotly argued political positions, Sealts had to admit disappointment. The hopes he and Hayford had cherished in their "Perspectives for Criticism" have been unfulfilled, for the simple reason that almost no one in a quarter century or more stopped, before writing on *Billy Budd, Sailor*, to read and master the interpretive significance of the information in the Chicago edition:

> With regard to the *Billy Budd* manuscript itself, both scholars and critics have too often neglected to go behind any and all reading texts of the story; there is still a need to acknowledge and assimilate what the Chicago Genetic Text and the accompanying editorial analysis have to tell them about Melville's art and Melville's thought as his story gradually took form. (425)

The point Sealts makes with such restraint, of course, is that scholars and critics alike have too often acted as if his and Hayford's edition were irrelevant to criticism.

As was already clear when Sealts wrote, the New Critical attitude toward authorial intention had dominated a succession of theoretical approaches to literature since the 1950s—including phenomenology, structuralism, and deconstruction. In the 1980s it conspicuously dominated the New Historicism, an approach which (contrary to its self-bestowed name) avoids historical, biographical, and textual research. This Marxist-derived approach denies that a literary work is created by an individual author's mind but instead sees a work as being "generated" by a social context. (New Historicists who treat textual matters see a printed text as the result of a process of "socialization" in which the editor or publisher or others are at least as important as the author.) These theorists acknowledge that their dread of being influenced by the power of an individual creative artist forces them to devise strategies for being sure that they can control the text. (For a patient account of this very popular 1980s literary approach see Edward Pechter, "The New Historicism and Its Discontents: Politicizing Renaissance Drama," *PMLA* 102 [May 1987]: 292-303.) To be ideologically consistent a New Historicist might be expected to champion *Billy Budd, Foretopman* (in one or another text), but none has done so: *Billy Budd, Sailor* had become sufficiently established as the standard text before the rise of the New Historicism, which tends to defend whatever is at the moment the most widely available text. Even more obviously, no New Historicist will find it necessary to engage the intricacies of the Genetic Text of *Billy Budd, Sailor*, since to follow the motions of Melville's mind through his revisions would be to acknowledge rather than repress authorial meaning.

Until recently to undertake to write a literary history was to commit oneself to research in literary history; in political, social, and cultural history; in biography; in textual scholarship; in bibliography—to the exploration of a great range of evidence in an attempt to tell the truth (or part of the truth) about conditions in the past. The New Historicists are perfecting a new academic genre, literary history without research, where the literary historian "is not a truthteller but a storyteller," the claim (p. xvii) by General Editor Emory Elliott in the introduction to the *Columbia Literary History of the United States* (New York: Columbia University Press, 1988). In the spirit of this introduction the author of the Melville chapter in that book, Robert Milder, ignores all new documentary discoveries about Melville (even the rich trove of papers acquired by the New York Public Library in 1983), yet begins with this intrinsically biographical sentence: "Reading Herman Melville in his fullness means attending to the peremptory inward development that impelled his most ambitious books, strained the confines of his literary forms, and gave his career an organic unity that subsumes and transcends the cumulative achievement of his works" (429). Here the New Critical version of the old notion of organic unity has been extrapolated from literary work to biography, even though Melville's own career suffered violent truncation rather than anything that obviously resembles an organic progression. Milder acknowledges the fact that a reliable edition of *Billy Budd* did not appear "until the Hayford-Sealts edition of 1962, long after *Billy Budd* criticism had taken shape" (446), but rather than engaging the problematical nature of the book and the criticism he concludes with a sonorous pronouncement which recalls the enthusiasts of the 1920s: Melville "has finished with the world and seems at the last to have dissolved the tortures of metaphysics and reputation in a conviction of inner sufficiency that is the closest he ever approached to peace" (447).

In the introduction to his *Critical Essays on Melville's "Billy Budd, Sailor"* (Boston: G. K. Hall, 1989), Robert Milder acknowledges "that *Billy Budd* lacks unity in the strict New Critical sense" (16), but denies that a reason for the lack of unity is the fact that it is unfinished. In making this claim Milder attempts to distinguish between "New Critical unity," which he sees as spatial ("a simultaneous grasp of one's materials in their complex interrelationship") and another (unnamed) sort of unity which he sees as temporal ("a disposition to allow one subject or theme to evolve from another, so that the coherence of the work came to reside in the process of thought that guided its unfolding and was visible in the fault lines of the product") (16). Milder does not confront the possibility that his concept of temporal unity could justify any author's maundering from topic to topic, and he evades the specific problems created for the reader who (if he or she is holding the Reading Text of *Billy Budd)* does not encounter the supposedly unifying sequence of topics in anything like the order in which Melville produced them (or the sequence in which he altered them). To read *Billy Budd* according to Milder's idea of temporal unity could lead to great insights about Melville's mental processes, but it would require a heroic attempt to read the Hayford-Sealts Genetic Text so as to recapture, however imperfectly, the sequence of Melville's labors, starting with the ballad. It would require the reader to comprehend the gross stages of the story's development as well as the sequence of alterations of words and phrases in particular passages, alterations made in stages difficult (and sometimes impossible) to identify. However tinged they are with wishful thinking, Milder's arguments deserve attention as evidence of just how determined modern academic critics are to discover an operative principle of unity in any work—even while they avoid direct engagement with biographical-textual evidence

such as Hayford and Sealts offer in the Genetic Text of *Billy Budd,
Sailor*. I cannot in this little book reverse the direction of a quarter-
century of criticism, but I can try, in the "Reading" which follows,
to make a start at acknowledging and assimilating the implications
of the Hayford-Sealts Genetic Text of the Chicago edition.

# A Chapter-by-Chapter Reading of *Billy Budd, Sailor*

### THE PLOT OF *BILLY BUDD* AND
### THE POLITICS OF INTERPRETING IT

The plot of *Billy Budd* is painful and to some even repellent. There will always be admirers of Melville who fervently wish he had abandoned the manuscript in 1889 in order meet the request of the London publisher Edward Garnett that he write the story of his early adventures. Instead, he continued to revise and rearrange many short poems and to rework his story of an innocent young seaman, Billy Budd, who, falsely accused by the master-at-arms, John Claggart, and unable to defend himself through speech, instinctively strikes out and kills his accuser in the presence of his captain, Edward Vere, who at once intuits the essential truth of the situation and (also at once) decides that the boy must be hanged. In rapid sequence the captain leads (or coerces) a hastily convened court martial to conclude what he wants it to conclude, then in a private meeting (to which the reader is denied access) reconciles the boy to his will, so that Billy blesses the captain as he is hanged. At his own death the captain murmurs the boy's name—without remorse.

The issues in this plot are momentous, and seem designed to force the reader to take one of two mutually incompatible positions. One is to agree with the captain that the preservation of law (even military law) overrules all considerations of natural law and justice. The other is to acknowledge that in this world those in power can and often do act as Vere did, but then to insist that Melville's story must be read as an attempt to rouse his readers to protest against any social institution which could sacrifice Billy Budd; such readers despise the captain who all-too-hastily makes his decision and cloaks it in a show of unanimity at a rigged court martial. Readers tend to assume that Melville must have felt about Vere just what they feel, even though other readers with equal conviction are sure that Melville meant just the opposite, and that *they* are the true understanders of the writer. Readers have bent Melville to their political ideologies, whatever they are. The more earnest interpretations of *Billy Budd*, to put it bluntly, are couched in fighting words. Those who disagree with us about the meaning of *Billy Budd* are people we would campaign hard against if they were running for public office; such people (unlike ourselves) are dangerous ideologues, however decorous their appearance and however plausible their language.

In this reading of the novel I will avoid the stance of an ideologue of the right or the left. The method in my reading is to focus on the story a chapter at a time, yet also to keep in mind what function any particular part of the story had when Melville wrote it and to ask, often, whether that part still retains all (or some of) the same function and (sometimes) if a part of the story has seemed to gain other functions. Rather than prescribing what subsequent critics should say, Hayford and Sealts were content to let readers follow the evidence wherever it led. In their brilliant questions (already quoted in the last paragraph of "*Billy Budd* as Late Masterpiece") they opened a series of possibilities which might be resolved by study of the Genetic Text—questions about how the quality of greatness emerged in *Billy Budd* and about the value of Melville's minute verbal revisions. Anyone during this last quarter century could have found in the Genetic Text thousands of pieces of evidence as to the vicissitudes of Melville's struggle to tell his story. Anyone could have found there the basic evidence as to whether or not Melville's revisions should be called a struggle to find the right word, the right phrase, or whether something else, less consciously controlled and less praiseworthy, was going on as Melville worked and reworked his prose, yet the following reading is the first full tour through *Billy Budd* to be conducted with regular (though by no means exhaustive) reference to the Hayford and Sealts Genetic Text as well as to their Reading Text. I re-emphasize that my comments in the following pages are initial garnerings from the treasure trove of information in the Genetic Text, a trove any adventuresome student can still encounter in an almost unplundered state.

## STARTING AT THE END (THE BALLAD)

The adventuresome student of *Billy Budd, Sailor* can best understand how Melville worked if he or she (having *read* the story in the Hayford-Sealts Reading Text) turns now to the ballad that concludes the story, "Billy in the Darbies," but which was (in its original form) the first part to be written. While Melville altered the ballad in many details between the time he drafted it around 1885 and his death, the ballad in its final form is still close to what it was when he first imagined the situation of a sailor waiting through the night for his execution on a charge (mutiny?) of which he was apparently guilty ("Ay, ay, all is up"). The poem is in the crude style which Melville favored in some other narrative sea-poems he was writing about the same time, perhaps in a self-conscious playing with the crudeness of nautical verse familiar from his seagoing years. (Melville *could* write better poetry than "Billy in the Darbies," so without leaping to the assumption that he was employing an aesthetic of calculated clumsiness we should assume that at least some of what we see as its awkwardnesses may be deliberate.) When you focus on the simplicity of the poem you will be in a better position to understand that when Melville began to write a headnote for it, as he did with other such poems, it took him a while to think his way past the situation he had committed himself to (the meditations of a guilty sailor, apparently not so young as Billy) into the beginnings of a story where the main character is an extraordinary—and altogether innocent—youth. You may come to understand why there is an awkwardness in the first two chapters, even after Melville had reworked them several times: they may still bear the marks of his halting, shifting attempts to develop a narrative from the poem even while he was becoming altogether more fascinated by his own erratically returning memories of the type of seaman known as the Handsome Sailor, and by his new character of Billy Budd who arose out of his prose different from the Billy of the poem.

Hayford and Sealts show that as his headnote expanded Melville wrote out Billy's story up to the point where he became the object of the master-at-arm's intense interest; then his attention for some time shifted to Claggart. Even if we start with the ballad and then read the first several chapters in order, we do not quite read the story in the sequence in which Melville wrote it. Instead, as we read the first part of the story we encounter interpolations placed down among more or less rewritten sections surviving from early stages. Some chapters placed after the Nelson "digression," for instance, were written before it. As you read the following pages you will want to keep in mind some of the effects that resulted from Melville's interpolating sections into parts already written, and you may well want to work out certain specific effects by resorting to the Genetic Text. It is impossible to talk with assurance about any reading of almost any chapter of *Billy Budd* without working through the Genetic Text for yourself. Let's put the situation bluntly: few topics important enough to treat in a term paper or a critical essay can be pursued honestly and rigorously without frequent recourse to the Genetic Text. People who write about almost any aspect of *Billy Budd* without working through the Genetic Text are pretty much wasting their time, or at least wasting pretty much of their time, however plausible their essays may seem.

### MELVILLE'S FIRST (AND FALTERING) PROSE (CHS. 1-2)

Only one leaf survives from the earliest stage of the draft of the headnote to the ballad, Melville's first work on the prose part of *Billy Budd*. This leaf, which Hayford and Sealts date to around 1885 or (at the latest) early 1886, is in pencil, a heavily rewritten single sentence repunctuated into two sentences (H-S 275) dealing with Billy Budd ("a rollicking seaman," nicknamed "Handsome," or "Beauty," or "The Jewel"); with his "genial" temper; with his features, frame, and bearing (which indicate "no ignoble lineage"); and with the fact that he, in "war time, Captain of a gun's crew in a seventy-four, is summarily condemned at sea to be hung as the ringleader of an incipient mutiny the spread of which was apprehended." In the earliest surviving parts of the final manuscript Melville has already moved beyond his focus on Billy as "Handsome" to the type of the Handsome Sailor (a type to which Billy Budd more or less belongs) and to the fact of his impressment (merely stated, not dramatized).

Before beginning a reading of chapters 1 and 2, I want to make a special appeal for patience and tolerance, first with me then with the story. It will seem that I am very slow and confused in getting started, and it may seem that I am disrespectful toward the author. Remember what Hayford and Sealts show in the Genetic Text: when Melville drafted the first chapter *he did not know where he would be going,* and he never went *back* to incorporate his full subsequent purposefulness into these chapters (insofar as his purposefulness ever became or remained "full"). So I beg for your tolerance with what I see as a necessarily slow introduction to a chapter-by-chapter reading of the story, and beg that you spare some of that tolerance for the great old writer who in the ballad and for a while after he began the headnote to the ballad was not yet writing greatly again after so many years of not writing great prose. As well as anyone, he knew (as he had said in the title piece to *The Piazza Tales*, 1856) that to embark on a heroic literary voyage was to go "where path was none, and none might go but by himself, and only go by daring." It took Melville a while to get his footing again on that pathless journey toward literary grandeur.

Chapter 1 at once launches the reader into the fluctuations of the narrator's consciousness, where one time in the past jostles against another time in the past, and one remote place collides with another remote place. Indeed, "the time before steamships" in the first sentence (43)—the time before the beginning of the nineteenth century—jostles also against the year 1843 specified in the dedication as the year Melville served with Jack Chase in the U.S. frigate *United States*. The dedication moves out of 1843 through the nearly half century subsequent to it and through this world and the next, for Melville does not know where that great heart, his hero and friend, "may now be," whether "Here on Earth or harbored in Paradise." (The dedication was probably written late, perhaps when Melville thought he was finished; it is inscribed on the reverse of a discarded page of what became chapter 21. See

H-S 383 and the first entry on 430, "Leaves with Inscribed Versos.")

At the start of chapter 1 qualifications almost overrun assertions. "In the time before steamships, or then more frequently than now," the story begins, locating the reader between the last decade of the eighteenth century and the "now" of the late 1880s—a stretch of some nine decades or a century—and then retreating from overassertion: if the sight to be described was not restricted to the time before steamships, at least it was more common then than now. The specified vantage point for regarding the spectacle is that of a civilian stroller along the docks, not a sailor, and the sight is that of a group of bronzed seamen flanking "some superior figure of their own class," of the type known as the "Handsome Sailor." The wording retreats from claiming the sight was witnessed in the past only "more frequently than now," for the Handsome Sailor seems to belong exclusively to that "less prosaic time alike of the military and merchant navies," the time before steamships, or at most the time not long after steamships were invented. The narrator commits himself to a belief that the present is more prosaic than the 1790s and is also more prosaic than the 1830s, for he recalls from the Liverpool of the middle past ("now half a century ago") a lustrous black Handsome Sailor he saw "under the shadow of the great dingy street-wall of Prince's Dock (an obstruction long since removed)." Wayfarers, strollers, whose attention was arrested by the barbaric son of Ham in Liverpool rendered spontaneous tributes of "a pause and stare, and less frequently an exclamation" (43-44); here "less frequently" reminds us of the opening "more frequently" in this time-saturated prose. Furthermore, the parenthetical comment about the obstruction long since removed introduces a fourth time, not only the 1790s, the late 1880s, and 1839, but also some indefinite date between the 1840s or 1850s and the present, the time when the street-wall (or, the untraveled reader may wonder, the Dock itself?) was removed. (1839 is the date of Melville's first stay at Liverpool. In a story in which the 1843 of the dedication locates Melville in autobiography and nineteenth-century history, there seems no good reason not to take the reference to Prince's Dock as autobiographical, and indeed there seems no aesthetic loss at this point if we talk of the narrator and Melville almost interchangeably.)

The first paragraph implied that a description would be given that would arrest the attention of the reader as strongly as the spectacle of the Handsome Sailor arrested the attention of the stroller along the docks, and the second paragraph delivers a splendid depiction of barbaric majesty on rollicking parade. (Hayford and Sealts show [243] that the description of the Negro and his white shipmates was an afterthought.) But the reader is also arrested by the compulsion of the narrator to move in and out of times and places, for the sailors surrounding the black Handsome Sailor were diverse enough to have been "marched up by Anacharsis Cloots before the bar of the first French Assembly as Representatives of the Human Race" (43). Paris of 1790 is superimposed over Liverpool of 1839, and the adjective "first" reminds the reader of bloody years in intervening French history, 1848 and 1871.

The first two paragraphs, then, accustom the reader to dual impulses—one Melville's desire as narrator to portray a remarkable human type, the barbaric Handsome Sailor surrounded by his worshiping shipmates, the other to let himself experience and then to record the motions of the mind through almost three quarters of a century of personal memory and another quarter century or more of history so vivid in his mind that he might almost have been witness to it.

The third paragraph begins "To return" (44), apparent evidence that Melville felt that he has developed the particular scene in Liverpool far enough if not almost too far. He wants now to make yet another distinction: the Handsome Sailor might well bedeck himself with enormous earrings and other finery (self-consciously displaying genuine unselfconscious joy in himself), but he was no mere effeminate dandy such as the "Billy-be-Dam," another character type which in the late 1880s is "all but extinct," although "occasionally to be encountered" at a duty which is, to real seamen, a joke: managing the tiller of boats on that strenuous challenge to nautical skill, the Erie Canal, or (still less heroically) "vaporing" (bombastically boasting) in the sordid barrooms along the towpath. The coherence threatens to fade away under the pen as the narrator yields to his desire to explain not only what the Handsome Sailor was but what he was not: not a Billy-be-Dam, a type which was never more than a parody of the real type. It seems that the real type, the "original," is the Handsome Sailor, but that reading turns out to be dubious. The Handsome Sailor was never simply amusing—arresting, but not amusing. More likely, Melville by the phrase "in a form yet more amusing than the original" meant "in a form of the Billy-be-Dam which is still further debased than the original Billy-be-Dam." Even so, taking "original" as a reference to the more or less pristine type of the Billy-be-Dam cannot solve the problem which follows, for the next pronoun ("he was also more or less of a mighty boxer or wrestler") has to refer to the Handsome Sailor.

Here is a transcription from the Genetic Text (283), an attempt to approximate what Melville had after he worked on the passage late in 1888 (not the way it stood at his death, after subsequent revisions):

> If in some cases a bit of a nautical Murat in setting forth his person ashore, the white forecastle-magnate of the period in question evinced nothing of that spurious sea-fop Billy-be-Dam, an amusing character all but extinct now, but occasionally to be encountered at the tiller of the boats on the tempestuous Erie Canal or, more likely, vaporing in the groggeries along the towpath. Invariably a proficient in his perilous calling, he was also more or less of a mighty boxer or wrestler. Ashore he was the champion; afloat the spokesman. Always foremost.

Melville wanted to expatiate on the type of the spurious sea-fop or Billy-be-Dam—not just to mention his existence but to speculate about the possible survival of a degenerate form of that already spurious type. The expatiation runs away with the sense, for the reader attentive to what he is being told about the Billy-be-Dam expects the next sentence to be about that amusing character type, and at first takes the "he" in "he was also more or less of a mighty boxer or wrestler" as the Billy-be-Dam. Then the reader is bewildered and makes the necessary correction, for the following sentences cannot be read unless the "he" is the Handsome Sailor. At this stage, when he did not really know where he was going, Melville let the power of his memory of the Erie Canal and his pleasure in elaborating the degeneration of a type of Canaller cloud his sense of what was most appropriate in the context. The mention of the Erie Canal seems merely personal, an American allusion which does not advance the portrait of the Handsome Sailor. (We know from chapter 54 of *Moby-Dick* that Canallers were powerful in Melville's memory and imagination—types of sybaritic sexuality combined with physical strength in a near-outlaw occupation.)

The "To return" looks for all the world like an indication that Melville thought he had strayed from business in the second paragraph and needed to get back to it. In fact, this phrase was a late addition, written after the development of the Billy-be-Dam passage. It may well indicate Melville's edginess about the relation of that Billy-be-Dam passage to anything that went before. In late revision Melville removed some of the connection (already weak enough) between the "Murat" and Billy-be-Dam passage and the foregoing passage, dropping the explicit contrast between the "intensely black" son of Ham and the "white forecastle-magnate." At this time he also sacrificed the alliteration of "spurious sea-fop" for the alliteration of "dandified Billy-be-Dam." After the revealingly apologetic "To return" the syntax gives no clue that the narrator is worried that his control over the story may be leaking away, and after leaving the Billy-be-Dam behind he focuses more sharply on the Handsome Sailor, always more or less "a mighty boxer or wrestler," always heroic, and focuses on a new aspect of the phenomenal character type: "The moral nature was seldom out of keeping with the physical make" (44). At last Melville is ready to introduce the "welkin-eyed Billy Budd," who must be a type of the Handsome Sailor, and who surely is such a cynosure of all eyes, at least in "aspect" (appearance) and partly if not wholly ("something such") in nature, "though with important variations made apparent as the story proceeds" (44). The foregoing paragraphs seem to have been building toward the presentation of Billy Budd as the particular Handsome Sailor whose story will be told here, but Melville does not let the case become so clear and simple: Billy is a variation of the type, not a perfect example of the Handsome Sailor.

And the narrator again moves into the past—the years "toward the close of the last decade of the eighteenth century," "hurried days" for British warships, when ships might put to sea short of hands (44-45). Those years comprise two different times, the earlier time of Billy's impressment and the slightly later time of the events of the story. Once again Melville's historical memory moves here and there—from England to France and from Scotland to

Philadelphia. The reader's reward for polite attentiveness comes in the second half of the chapter, the story of Billy's impressment by Lieutenant Ratcliffe of H.M.S. *Bellipotent* from Captain Graveling's *Rights-of-Man*, so named because her "hardheaded Dundee owner was a staunch admirer of Thomas Paine." In the less prosaic time around the end of the eighteenth century ideas were worth fighting for. Paine's "book in rejoinder to Burke's arraignment of the French Revolution had then been published for some time and had gone everywhere" (48). The scene in which the lieutenant steadily drinks his way through the captain's story of the way Billy drubbed Red Whiskers and brought peace to the ship is a vividly comic way of preparing us to expect sudden violent action from a phenomenally patient young man. It also introduces what was through most of the period of the composition a major theme of the story: the likelihood that human actions will be misunderstood—and not necessarily to one's disadvantage, as it would be in many a farce, melodrama, or tragedy. Billy's farewell to the ship ("And good-bye to you too, old *Rights-of-Man*") was uttered without satire, Billy being one of those human beings who cannot deal in double meanings, even in jest (49). The lieutenant takes it as satire, but apparently he does not dislike the spirit which he perceives in it; nor, we learn later, does Vere, who also misunderstands the spirit in which Billy had bade farewell.

In chapter 2 Melville works his way from comparative simplicity (however hesitantly presented) to new complexities. The first distinction is between Billy's former prominence in merchant ships and his position on the man-of-war as hardly the "cynosure he had previously been" (50). Melville ponders the reason that Billy was not abashed at the transition: conceit or vanity might have made him abashed, and he possessed neither of those vices. He is wholly unselfconscious as to others' responses to his "person and demeanor," qualities which forcefully strike the "more intelligent gentlemen of the quarter-deck" (51). Drawing on conventional notions of what the pure Saxon strain might have been like, then comparing Billy to a statue of Hercules by a Greek sculptor, Melville reads in Billy's delicate features "something suggestive of a mother eminently favored by Love and the Graces" (51), and hints that the foundling Billy was "a presumable by-blow, and, evidently, no ignoble one. Noble descent was as evident in him as in a blood horse" (52). The chapter becomes an extended analysis of Billy not as example of Handsome Sailor but as an extraordinary human being, one who is as ignorant of evil as Adam before the Fall. Billy has had sexual experience, Melville strongly implies, "frank manifestations in accordance with natural law" (52), but such experience has posed no threat to his innocence or unselfconsciousness.

Visualizing Billy as "a sort of upright barbarian," like Adam before "the urbane Serpent wriggled himself into his company" (52), Melville calls a halt in his analysis in order to devote a paragraph to his views on nature and civilization. His voice is that of a survivor from another age, one which took the possibility of Original Sin seriously. The "doctrine of man's Fall" is "now popularly ignored" (52), yet corroborating that unfashionable doctrine are a series of observations Melville makes about pristine virtues when they appear in one who wears "the external uniform of civilization" (53). Such virtues turn out "not to be derived from custom or convention," but anomalous, as if "transmitted from a period prior to Cain's city and citified man" (53). The reflection follows an earlier comparison of Billy on the man-of-war to a "rustic beauty" suddenly put among "highborn dames of the court" (51), but it does not seem altogether consistent with the previous insistence on Billy's noble blood. And the paragraph strays into mention of a celebrated pastless youth (the term popularized in the late twentieth century is "wild child"), Caspar Hauser, and from there into an application of lines from Martial's *Epigrams* to any inheritor of primitive virtues who arrives, all unprepared, in a city. The paragraph wanders off and is left dangling. It is indicative of the lack of control that the quotation from the Roman poet is not even anchored by subsequent authorial comment.

The next paragraph abruptly announces that Billy is "like the beautiful woman in one of Hawthorne's minor tales" ("minor" in the sense of "shorter") in having "just one thing amiss in him" (53). Unlike Georgiana's flaw in "The Birthmark," Billy's blemish is invisible, "an occasional liability to a vocal defect," a stutter which is the mark laid on him by "the arch interferer, the envious marplot of Eden" (53). The little paragraph which then concludes the chapter submits this "imperfection in the Handsome Sailor" as evidence that Billy is "not presented as a conventional hero" and that "the story in which he is the main figure is no romance" (53).

In the first two chapters the reader has to watch the meaning seem to escape, then watch as Melville pulls it back within bounds. Melville writes as an old man with wonderful memories (his own and other people's) of many times and places, a man with opinions which may challenge the reader (who, especially if young, will hardly relish being told that the writer remembers a more poetic age than the young can now hope to experience), and a man who is going to tell his story in his own good time. Fumbling may well be evident in the first two chapters, and even more evident if you look at the Genetic Text, but Melville, old, tired, and intermittently sick and gradually weakening, was still a great writer. Much of that greatness asserted itself as he worked his way into his material, before the end of the second chapter.

## MELVILLE GATHERS HIS FORCES (CH. 3)

Chapter 3 marks a discovery (more than recovery?) of direction. The first paragraph defines the anomalous role of the *Bellipotent*—sometimes with the Mediterranean fleet, sometimes on separate duty, and as it happens on separate duty at both the time of Billy's impressment and the time of his execution. Melville defines the limits of his story: it has to do not with the maneuvers of the fleet but only with "the inner life of one particular ship and the career of an individual sailor" (54). (An excursus: The name of the ship through most of the composition of the story was the *Indomitable*. Hayford and Sealts emended all occurrences of *Indomitable* because Melville decided, at a late stage, to change the name, although he did not go back to make the change every time he had written *Indomitable*. One might expect that if a highly suggestive name had remained in the story for years then it might have been *built into* its language, perhaps by use of related words such as "domination," perhaps by alliteration near where the name of the ship occurs, and so one might fruitfully study the Genetic Text for evidence that some such allusiveness might have been lost from the text by the author's late change and the editors' wholly justified editorial policy of adopting the new name throughout.)

Here in chapter 3 for the first time Melville dates the action to the summer of 1797 and defines what he had meant earlier by "hurried days," the time following the rebellion at Spithead (April) and the Nore (May). In this passage he defines the Great Mutiny in a voice like that of Edmund Burke, not Thomas Paine: the bluejackets who ran the British colors up the flagstaff with the union and cross wiped out had "by that cancellation" transmuted "the flag of founded law and freedom defined, into the enemy's red meteor of unbridled and unbounded revolt" (54). Melville's point of view at this point is clear—that of a traditionalist, a deeply conservative man apprehensive at the thought that insurrection might shake England, which was then "all but the sole free conservative" power "of the Old World" (54). We are told that some of the demands made by the mutineers at the Nore were deemed by the authorities as "not only inadmissible but aggressively insolent" (55). Rather than focusing on the injustices toward sailors, Melville is interested in, and appalled by, the French-inspired irrational combustion into which those grievances were ignited, then he focuses on the fact that the Great Mutiny is one of the suppressed episodes of history, one about which information is hard to come by, even "in the libraries" (55). We know the sort of thing he has in mind from his comments in *Clarel* (pt. 4, canto 9, "The Shepherds' Dale") about America's own national sins, memory of which has been suppressed—the North's blockade which kept medicines from the South during the Civil War, for example, and similar episodes in American history which "national pride along with views of policy would fain shade" into "the historical background" (55). Comparing the Nore Mutiny to a contagious fever thrown off by a healthy body (but not insisting on that comparison), Melville closes the chapter with the reminder that among the thousands of mutineers were some who (from whatever motive) "helped to win a coronet for Nelson at the Nile, and the naval crown of crowns for him at Trafalgar," those battles being "a plenary absolution and a grand one": "For all that goes to make up scenic naval display and heroic magnificence in arms, those battles, especially Trafalgar, stand unmatched in human annals" (56).

Now a reminder about specific problems with what was taken as the "preface" until the Hayford-Sealts edition. In chapter 3 the reference to the year 1797 was already written (244) before Melville wrote what was later mistaken as a preface (259). That is to say, the opening of that much-quoted passage, "The year 1797, the year of this narrative" (377), was not intended as new exposition—instead, it was (when it stood in what became chapter 19) an explicit reminder to the reader of the earlier mention here in chapter 3. And Melville's reference (in the second paragraph of that discarded section) to what had been "elsewhere hinted" (378) was not a prefatory glance toward something yet to be read but a backward glance at what was already written, here in chapter 3.

## THE PROBLEMATICAL ROLE OF LORD NELSON (CHS. 4-5)

Chapter 4 focuses the difficulty of interpreting the story as no earlier section does. Melville starts (in a beginning which was a later addition) with a confession of sin but with no real sign that he is repentant: indeed, he invites us to sin along with him. The problem he articulates at the outset is that he finds it hard to keep to the main road and off some enticing bypaths. That seems honest enough, when we recall, most glaringly, his allowing himself to be lured up that distracting towpath in chapter 1. But this luring the reader into complicity is a literary device of high sophistication, not a plea that incoherence may be ignored. (Contrast this sophistication with that hapless "To return" in chapter 1.)

Melville's broodings about the differences between the times he has witnessed break out now into an essay on the rapidity of change in sea warfare in "our time" (56). In "Bridegroom-Dick," one of the poems in *John Marr* (1888), Melville made it clear that although he had lived into "a lubber's day" he could still remember the days before "the Old Order foundered." Here as narrator of *Billy Budd* Melville observes more complexly that there are few who "can hold the Present at its worth without being inappreciative of the Past," and as one of those few he celebrates the solitary hulk of Lord Nelson's *Victory* anchored at Portsmouth, "a poetic reproach" to the ironclads which have replaced her as the most modern warships (57). Nelson loomed large for all nineteenth-century British and American seamen, and for Melville the thought of him involved complex associations. In 1839 Melville saw many times the statuary group near the Liverpool docks depicting Nelson's death-in-victory, and he looked at it again on 8

November 1856 "with peculiar emotion," as he put it in his journal, remembering not only his youthful study of it but also his detailed use of it in chapter 31 of *Redburn* (1849). On 21 November 1849 Melville visited the Nelson Room at the Greenwich Hospital, where Lord Nelson's body had lain in state, and saw there much memorabilia, including the coat Nelson wore at the Battle of the Nile and the one he wore when he received his death wound at Trafalgar ("coats of Nelson in glass cases," he noted in his journal). On Christmas of that year Melville saw the *Victory* "at anchor" at Portsmouth. During the intervening years the seeming loss of heroic virtues in war and in peace had combined to exalt that noble ship in his imagination. In *Battle-Pieces* (1866) Melville had brooded upon the changes in naval warfare between the days of Nelson and the days of the first battling ironclads, the *Monitor* and the *Merrimac*. He had devoted one poem, "The Temeraire," to the ship which followed Nelson's *Victory* into battle at Trafalgar, and in another poem he took (for dramatic purposes) "A Utilitarian View of the Monitor's Fight." Here in chapter 4 the narrator is not one of the "martial utilitarians" (57) who measure a weapon only by its efficiency in preserving the lives of one's own side while killing as many enemies as possible: the ship *Victory* and Nelson himself both embodied non-utilitarian values. Melville's grounds are partly aesthetic—the ironclads are unsightly. His other reasons for seeing the *Victory* as a poetic reproach to the ironclads remain unstated as he develops a hypothetical argument. There may be some who share his sense of the meaning of the "solitary old hulk" (57) yet who adhere to the new order. These hypothetical persons then display themselves as "martial utilitarians," the "Benthamites of war" (57), who would condemn Nelson for a foolhardy and vainglorious display at Trafalgar which caused his death and then led to the deaths of many men because he was not alive to guide them safely through the tempest which followed the battle.

In *Billy Budd* as in *Battle-Pieces* Melville's view is clearly opposed to that of the martial utilitarians: "Personal prudence, even when dictated by quite other than selfish considerations, surely is no special virtue in a military man; while an excessive love of glory, impassioning a less burning impulse, the honest sense of duty, is the first" (58). Furthermore, Melville ends the chapter with a rhetorically exalted tribute to Nelson's preparations for battle and death: "if thus to have adorned himself for the altar and the sacrifice were indeed vainglory, then affectation and fustian is each more heroic line in the great epics and dramas, since in such lines the poet but embodies in verse those exaltations of sentiment that a nature like Nelson, the opportunity being given, vitalizes into acts" (58).

Having written such a passionate (and coherent) chapter, Melville removed it from the manuscript around the end of 1888. He never actually reinserted it (though in a cleaning-up phase he allowed page numbers for it). He wrote it before he developed the character of Vere. He removed it even before he began to elaborate the characterization of Vere (245-46). After he began that elaboration, the passage apparently became even more problematical in his mind—not just because it was a digression but, very likely, because he sensed or saw that it set up a standard of comparison against which Vere would inevitably be measured, and against which Vere would always come short. Melville composed for what is now chapter 7 a reported compliment to Captain Vere, the assertion that Sir Horatio (as Nelson was called at that point) "is at bottom scarce a better seaman or fighter" (63). But any impulse of ours to argue that this compliment is strong evidence that Melville meant us to see Vere as like Nelson, not unlike him, must be checked by the reminder that chapter 7 also, like the Nelson chapter, was kept out of the manuscript, in a separate folder; on the cover of this folder Melville wrote: "*About / Captain Vere / To be inserted after first account of him.*" Why Melville kept this chapter on Vere out of the manuscript is not clear. Hayford and Sealts suggest (248) that he could not decide where to insert it, but they also show that probably it had been somewhat longer before Melville cannibalized parts of it. An oddity is that this other chapter also kept out of the manuscript contains the only passage which explicitly compares Vere to Nelson. In any case, whatever he felt about what is now chapter 7, Melville may well have felt that chapter 4, the Nelson chapter, was simply too good to throw away, even though he may have had a strong impulse to sacrifice it for the good of larger relationships of part to part.

The New Critic cannot help us much with chapter 4 since he or she will expect any part of a work to function significantly in relation to the rest of the work. If an author lavishes a chapter upon Lord Nelson then Nelson is plainly of very high importance, and since he has almost nothing to do with Billy, Claggart, Graveling, the Dansker, or any other character except Captain Vere (who is like Nelson a sailor of high rank and also like Nelson a man of phenomenal personal qualities), then he must have been put into the story in order to provide a parallel for Captain Vere, a standard by which to judge his behavior. The New Critic would very cheerfully assign a class to write a paper on "The Function of the Nelson Chapter in *Billy Budd*"—an impossible topic unless grounded in information in the Genetic Text.

The composition of the part of chapter 5 that deals with the mutinies and impressment probably followed directly after chapter 3; the Nelson passages were added later, at the time the Nelson chapter was written (246). Here at the start of chapter 5 Melville acknowledges that "not every grievance" of the mutineers at the Nore was subsequently "redressed" (58). The war contractors were checked in "some" (by no means all) of their cheating practices, but impressment continued, on the grounds of necessity: the navy could not be kept afloat without impressing seamen. Dwelling briefly on the discontent which survived the "Two Mutinies" (59), the Spithead as well as the already specified Nore, Melville gives an instance of naval apprehensiveness which again exalts the character of Nelson. In 1797 Nelson's command was changed so that he could be on the *Theseus*, whose men had mutinied. Nelson, it was thought, could win them to service "by force of his mere presence and heroic personality" (59). So while the chapter adequately establishes that commanders in the months after the mutinies had reason to be fearful, it also asserts that an extraordinary leader like Nelson could sway a rebellious crew to loyalty. Though Melville removed chapter 4, he left in chapter 5 without deleting this tribute to Nelson. So even with chapter 4 removed (as it was from late 1888 onward) the manuscript still contained these references to the extraordinary commander whose example would force any reader to judge Vere's subsequent behavior against the standard set by Nelson.

## LATE-WRITTEN PREPARATORY SCENES (CHS. 6-7)

Chapters 6 and 7, Hayford and Sealts show (247), were written late, Melville's "object being to prepare the reader for those later scenes already drafted," earlier-written scenes including not only the description of Claggart's accusation of Billy to Vere and Billy's killing Claggart in Vere's presence but also the trial scene, written shortly *before* chapters 6 and 7. The first of these two late-written chapters, chapter 6, is devoted to establishing Captain Vere as an altogether admirable commander, "mindful of the welfare of his men, but never tolerating an infraction of discipline; thoroughly versed in the science of his profession, and intrepid to the verge of temerity, though never injudiciously so" (60). The reader coming to this passage after the earlier discussions of Nelson cannot help weighing Vere against the heroic Nelson and finding that he comes somewhat short by being judicious when Nelson could display an "excessive love of glory" (58), not personal prudence.

Chapter 7, written like chapter 6 at a stage *after* the later trial scene was composed and while the Nelson chapter was removed to a separate folder (247-48), seems wholly admiring toward Vere. The problem for the reader who has already encountered chapter 4 in the printed text is that Vere is being presented as almost as admirable as Nelson, and therefore a man from whom more than caution (resorted to as if by reflex action) should be expected in time of crisis. The depiction of Vere's taste in reading also sounds very much like Melville's own taste, an indication that not much distance will be marked between the author and the character:

> With nothing of that literary taste which less heeds the thing conveyed than the vehicle, his bias was toward those books to which every serious mind of superior order occupying any active post of authority in the world naturally inclines: books treating of actual men and events no matter of what era—history, biography, and unconventional writers like Montaigne, who, free from cant and convention, honestly and in the spirit of common sense philosophize upon realities. (62)

His reading of such serious books reconfirms in Vere his already settled convictions, which were "as a dike against those invading waters of novel opinion social, political, and otherwise" (62) that overwhelmed many minds in that Revolutionary period. Aloof from the trivialities of the present, apt to draw parallels from history rather than contemporary examples, he shares some of Melville's own superior reserve. The final tribute to "natures constituted like Captain Vere's" predisposes the reader to expect from him, in crisis, not only composure but self-confident daring, for the "honesty" in such natures "prescribes to them directness, sometimes far-reaching like that of a migratory fowl that in its flight never heeds when it crosses a frontier" (63).

## EARLIER-WRITTEN CLAGGART SCENES (CHS. 8-9)

As Melville wrote his way from mere headnote to story, he had followed his elaboration of Billy's history and character with an account of Claggart, also developed at some length, before he wrote any of the passages on Vere (249). Some of that later-written treatment of Vere precedes the introduction, in chapter 8, of Claggart (although particular content and phrasing in the Claggart chapters does not necessarily date from such an early stage). The point we need to keep in mind is that Melville invented Claggart and worked out the characterization of him before writing down much about the captain who would have to preside at the execution of his hero. At the outset of the chapter, Melville admits to the reader that he will never succeed at drawing Claggart's portrait. Before he makes his attempt at the portrait, he moves into still another of his descriptions of changes over a long history, this time the change in function of a master-at-arms. He moves from physical description of Claggart to rumors about his past, then relates the sailors' "dogwatch gossip" (65) concerning Claggart to factual history about the way London police filled out British naval rolls when necessary by arresting "any able-bodied suspect" (65) they chose. Recalling tales of men who enlisted as a way of evading punishment ashore, Melville appeals for confirmation to a book in which he read something of the sort, although he cannot recall what the book was. The effect of this apparently naive admission is oddly convincing. Lacking that bibliographical citation, Melville makes a still stronger appeal to personal knowledge based on a talk he had "more than forty years ago" (in 1849, for a journal entry seems to make it clear that this is autobiographical) on the terrace at Greenwich with "a Baltimore Negro, a Trafalgar man" (66)— an old man who had sailed under Nelson at Trafalgar! The story of England's desperate efforts to man its ships leads Melville at once into intense reflection which he wants the reader to share: if we agree it is true that many sailors on ships of Nelson's time were not merely impressed but were sometimes men released from jails to sea duty, then "how significant would it be of England's straits at the time confronted by those wars which like a flight of harpies rose shrieking from the din and dust of the fallen Bastille" (66).

What follows is a brilliant bringing to life of remote historical events, and more important, a rekindling of feelings intensely held by people now half a century or three quarters of a century dead. Here Melville sees it as fatuous to read about the Revolutionary era and think of it as "measurably clear" (66). Reading and eking out that research with a vivifying imagination might bring one closer to historical truth (though many stories are not to be found, we already know, even in libraries). Personal communication from an old man looking far back from the mid-century is more likely than books to convey a realizing sense of the past—a sense of horror at the French Revolution and the excesses which continued to follow it. Better still is it to remember the attitudes within your own family. In Melville's case "grandfathers of us graybeards, the more thoughtful of them" (66), is not meant to be precisely accurate, since he never saw his Gansevoort grandfather; rather, it applies to his Gansevoort uncles and great-uncles and his Melvill grandfather and uncle and their friends and associates (among whom was the deeply conservative Lemuel Shaw, who only a short time after the Great Mutinies was engaged to marry an aunt of Melville's and who long afterwards became Melville's father-in-law). As he wrote in the late 1880s, Melville's mind was a vault of memories of the terror Napoleon had struck in some Federalist American circles. And after this rapt passage Melville modulates into a brief analysis first of the limited notions of human iniquity held by the "sea quidnuncs" (67) who inveighed against Claggart as much for the unpopular office he occupied as for his personal qualities, then an analysis of Claggart's genius at manipulating both his superiors and his inferiors on the ship.

Chapter 8, written after Melville had worked his way far along in his portrayal of Billy Budd but before he had done much at all to characterize the captain (249), may profitably be compared with chapters 1 and 2, where my reading suggests that Melville fumbled his way from point to point. No fumbling here.

The depiction in chapter 9 of Billy's life in the foretop and the early signs of trouble dates from the earliest phases of the story, before Claggart was developed, before Vere was developed (250). Even the Dansker, Hayford and Sealts assume, was added after the initial inscription (250) as part of a pattern whereby Melville first worked up his descriptive passages then invented characters and action to dramatize the issues. Melville plainly took some grim pleasure in inventing a grizzled, skeptical old character not wholly unlike himself and took pains to link him to the embodiment of highest heroism, giving him (69) battle service with Nelson on the *Agamemnon* in 1795 (his scar is a trophy of his prowess on a boarding party). Rather than reading the Dansker's mind, Melville at first speculates about what could have produced his amusement at the sight of Billy Budd, then offers a reading of a subsequent stage of the Dansker's response to him, where the quizzing or teasing sort of look would sometimes be "replaced by an expression of speculative query as to what might eventually befall a nature like that, dropped into a world not without some mantraps and against whose subtleties simple courage lacking experience and address, and without any touch of defensive ugliness, is of little avail" (70). Here Melville is describing a character type that had long fascinated him, one he embodied most memorably in his portrait of the real Amasa Delano in "Benito Cereno." Such innocence does "not always sharpen the faculties or enlighten the will" in "a moral emergency" (70)—a sort of emergency Billy has never experienced. Continuing his pattern of describing Billy in classical or biblical terms, Melville here envisions the odd pair, the Dansker and Billy, as an "old sea Chiron" pausing in his tutoring of the "young Achilles" (71). The Dansker refuses to tutor Billy by elaborating on his blunt warning that "Jemmy Legs" (i.e., the master-at-arms) was responsible for the numerous small troubles Billy had experienced. Melville ran a danger in inventing a wise old character who immediately sees that Claggart is the source of Billy's harassment, for Captain Vere, when the time comes, may strike some readers as a trifle less perceptive than the old Dansker. But like Melville's other dramatizations, this one is effective: the reader finds it satisfying to see innocence offered the aid of truth gained from long experience, even if the innocent one rejects the truth so straightforwardly—if laconically—offered.

THE DANSKER—LATECOMER TO THE CLAGGART SCENES (CH. 10)

The content of chapter 10, the soup-spilling scene, may have been part of an earlier stage (251), but the just-invented Dansker governs the present form of chapter 10, for the new action confirms Billy in not believing the Dansker's warning. Melville recurs to the "misconstruing" theme, here the failure to understand the behavior of others. Claggart's "Handsomely done, my lad! And handsome is as handsome did it, too!" (72) strikes the other seamen as humorously meant, and they laugh because they know they are expected to; and Billy, complimented and relieved that the Dansker's suspicions are dispelled, joins merrily in the laughter. The little chapter passes through several distinct trouble zones: Claggart could reprimand Billy, unjustly, but does not; the episode, if it had been worked out another way, might have confirmed the Dansker's warning, but it does not; Billy's incautious blurting out that someone had told him Claggart was down on him could have resulted in some danger, but it does not.

The most memorable, and most blatant, parts of the chapter involve Melville's characterization of Claggart after he has suppressed his first reaction on recognizing Billy and has tapped Billy playfully on the bottom with his rattan and spoken the cheerful-sounding words to him. Billy does not see (and apparently no one else sees) "the involuntary smile, or rather grimace, that accompanied Claggart's equivocal words," a grimace that aridly "drew down the thin corners of his shapely mouth" (72). Then Claggart incautiously lets his face reveal some of his emotions:

> Meantime that functionary, resuming his path, must have momentarily worn some expression less guarded than that of the bitter smile, usurping the face from the heart—some distorting expression perhaps, for a drummer-boy heedlessly frolicking along from the opposite direction and chancing to come into light collision with his person was strangely disconcerted by his aspect. Nor was the impression lessened when the official, impetuously giving him a sharp cut with the rattan, vehemently exclaimed, "Look where you go!" (73)

The story weakens here into the one of the less worthy Hawthornesque modes. In *The Scarlet Letter*, chapter 3, a "writhing horror" twists itself across Chillingworth's features, "like a snake gliding swiftly over them," before he "so instantaneously" controls his powerful emotion "by an effort of his will" that except for a single moment his expression "might have passed for calmness," and those who peer after Hester Prynne in the prison whisper "that the scarlet letter threw a lurid gleam along the dark passage-way of the interior." Hawthorne was on Melville's mind (as the reference in chapter 2 shows), with ill effects, for the lurid changes of Claggart's countenance fit poorly with the realistic depiction of the dialogue between the Dansker and Billy in the previous chapter, or indeed with the realistic depiction of Billy and his friends in this chapter. This sort of thing is all right for Hawthorne, or for a tribute to Hawthorne, but it was never Melville's way, even when (as in *Moby-Dick*) he attempted to create his own version of the gothic satanic figure.

## EXPANSION OF THE PORTRAIT OF CLAGGART (CHS. 11-13)

Chapters 11, 12, and part of 13, Hayford and Sealts show (251-54), are a substantial expansion of an earlier treatment of Claggart. Melville's manner of expanding the story out of a headnote to the ballad was to introduce and elaborate one character at a time. An earlier form of these Claggart chapters preceded all of the longer passages on Vere, although now the reader encounters some important passages on Vere before the depiction of Claggart. Melville did not rewrite to include much in the way of comparative analysis of the characters. The brief contrast of Claggart and Billy at the start of chapter 12 is merely a means of focusing on the master-at-arms's motivating envy.

When in chapter 11 Melville asks at once: "What was the matter with the master-at-arms?" (73), the commonsensical question brushes past the melodramatic grimace at the end of the previous chapter. Confident of himself now (contrast his shaky start in the first two chapters), Melville recurs to his earlier observation that Billy is not the hero of a conventional romance. Just as it would have been easy for Melville to invent an episode in Captain Vere's past which would let us learn, to our profound astonishment, that, say, Vere was the father (or uncle, or friend of the father) of the beautiful baby left in a basket in Bristol, now it would be easy for him "to invent something touching the more private career of Claggart, something involving Billy Budd, of which something the latter should be wholly ignorant" (73), a quintessentially romantic (and specifically Dickensian) situation. And rather than being hopelessly sentimental, such a conventional plot line, Melville acknowledges, could be "more or less interesting" (73). Melville makes clear his distance from such romancings, for "in fact there was nothing of the sort":

> And yet the cause necessarily to be assumed as the sole one assignable is in its very realism as much charged with that prime element of Radcliffian romance, the mysterious, as any that the ingenuity of the author of *The Mysteries of Udolpho* could devise. For what can more partake of the mysterious than an antipathy spontaneous and profound such as is evoked in certain exceptional mortals by the mere aspect of some other mortal, however harmless he may be, if not called forth by this very harmlessness itself? (74)

This powerful passage overwhelms the following paragraph, which asks the reader to imagine how an antipathy would be aggravated by being confined with its object in the close limits of a ship, and admits that for the reader of "a normal nature" to comprehend Claggart more hints are needed, and the task best achieved by indirection.

Toward the middle of chapter 11 Melville recalls or invents "an honest scholar" (74), older than he and now dead, who long ago commented to him on the complexities of another man, also now dead, whose "labyrinth" was not to be explored with mere "knowledge of the world" (74). Here Melville makes himself the lone survivor of a trio, one so inexperienced at the time of the remembered conversation that he could not comprehend "the drift" (75) of the honest scholar's words, but now more experienced and perhaps wiser. Familiar knowledge of the world, when it takes the keenness off intuition, may in fact be a hindrance, it is suggested, to the understanding of "certain exceptional characters, whether evil ones or good" (75). All these years later, the narrator is more isolated than ever, left stranded in an alien age, and far too old to have (as Billy has in chapter 9) a living Chiron to his own Achilles:

> And, indeed, if that lexicon which is based on Holy Writ were any longer popular, one might with less difficulty define and

denominate certain phenomenal men. As it is, one must turn to some authority not liable to the charge of being tinctured with the biblical element. (75)

Melville's irony works more than one way. Always of a religious nature, as Hawthorne recorded after long talks with him amid the dunes at Southport in 1856, he had been accused of blasphemy by reviewers of *Moby-Dick*. Now Melville has so outlived his reckless youthful irreverence that he feels himself stranded outside his own age, having lived into a period in which biblical terms such as "sin" are no longer in the vocabulary of popular writers. Left among a generation which turns not to theology but to psychology for explanations of human behavior, Melville must seek out a kind of authority more in tune with the time, a Greek philosopher, Plato; but ironically what he finds in Plato (and by implication all serious thinkers) is a doctrine savoring of Calvinistic belief in the natural depravity of man (although it applies only to some individuals, not, like Calvinism, to all human beings).

The popular pseudoscience of psychology (flourishing long before Sigmund Freud's writings reached the United States) for once has yielded not a bland and reassuring formula (such as the 1880s equivalent of the assurance that Billy is OK and Claggart is OK) but something that sounds perplexingly and outrageously theological. Melville's hands of course are clean, for he has not committed the gaucherie of insisting that only theological terms can account for behavior as abnormal as Claggart's. It sounds as if the narrator is writing for an audience dissolving in front of his eyes. After the elaborate buildup suggested by Claggart's nature, Melville moves into a thoughtful analysis of a sort of controlled madness that can use even reason as "an ambidexter implement for effecting the irrational" (76), a topic which relates Claggart to Melville's Ahab of four decades in the past. The analysis leads Melville to class Claggart as mad in some such way and to reiterate, more strongly than before, that innate within him was "'a depravity according to nature.'" The reflection evokes a prideful sense of Melville's integrity in isolation: "Dark sayings are these, some will say. But why? Is it because they somewhat savor of Holy Writ in its phrase 'mystery of iniquity'? If they do, such savor was far enough from being intended, for little will it commend these pages to many a reader of today" (76). On such a topic Melville might, a few years before, have been unable to bring to bear such controlled irony. However isolated he may have felt as he wrote this passage, he knew that others were helping to hold back the tide of mediocrity and blandness. The British correspondents who mixed their admiration of him with admiration of Thomson and FitzGerald had given him back a small but staunch literary community to replace the imaginary companions he had resorted to in the Burgundy Club sketches, the maundering, irresolute creation of his starkest isolation. In his new self-confidence Melville does not offer even a facetious apology for a digressive passage: this chapter was "necessitated" (77) by the fact that the story turns on the hidden nature of Claggart.

Like chapter 11, chapter 12, which is devoted to analysis of Claggart's envy of Billy, underwent strenuous revision. It was composed late, *after* most of the treatment of Claggart's schemings, his false accusation of Billy, and his death (chs. 17-19). Early in 1889 Melville removed from the start of this chapter two leaves about the classes of people competent to testify in courts of law as expert witnesses, the first leaf bearing the chapter title, "Lawyers, Experts, Clergy." (See "Preservation and Transcription," above, and "Textual Problems Created by Weaver," below, as well as comments on chapters 16 and 26, below.) Hayford and Sealts praise Melville (254) for his "meticulous process of revising and recasting" the leaves of both chapter 11 and chapter 12, with this particular praise for his work on chapter 12: "Consistently he revises the elaborative pencil revision as he makes the fair copy; and for the final version he is working toward directness—pruning qualifications, compressing metaphors, and eliminating the allusions to Milton and Spenser" (that is, omitting the allusions to well-known passages where both writers personify Envy). These allusions deserve some attention, since they are arguably built into the chapter as Melville left it, although as he revised he cut the specific references, which had been so important that he considered "Pale ire, envy and despair" as a chapter title. (Had he lived, he might, for all we know, have given every chapter a title.) The Spenser allusion is from canto 4 of *The Faerie Queene*:

> . . . malicious Envie rode
> Upon a ravenous wolfe, and still did chaw

> Between his cankred teeth a venemous tode,
> Then all the poison ran about his jaw;
> But inwardly he chawed his own maw
> At neighbours wealth, that made him ever sad;
> For death it was, when any good he saw . . . .

Misremembering the sex of Spenser's Envy, Melville wrote "In his personification of envy, Spencer depicts her as a ghastly hag forever chewing a toad," and in revisions added "poisonous" before "toad" (340). He followed that passage with a comparison to the way the subject was treated by another English poet in whose works he had steeped himself over many years: "'Pale ire, envy, and despair' is Miltonic" (340). That passage (not marked in Melville's two-volume Milton which came to light in the early 1980s) is from book 4 of *Paradise Lost*, where Satan falls into self-doubt in Eden before confirming himself in evil (Melville's edition has a comma after "pale," making it a noun). Over Satan's face emotions pass in sequence just before he becomes (in the text of Melville's edition) "the first / That practis'd falshood under saintly shew, / Deep malice to conceal." As Melville cut these two explicit literary allusions he still left in the allusion to a biblical instance of envy, that of Saul toward David (which begins in I Samuel 18)—a story which seems to have infused his treatment of Radney and Steelkilt in chapter 54 of *Moby-Dick*, "The Town-Ho's Story." The submergence of literary allusions here nevertheless left Spenserian echoes (envy as a monster) and the Miltonic topic of the reactionary bite of the serpent (Melville knew the Latin meaning of "remorse") uncontrolled by the naming of the two great English poets. What Hayford and Sealts say about the suppression of explicit allusions here suggests that a scrutiny of the Genetic Text might lead to insights about the ease or the edginess with which Melville made all of his other literary, artistic, and historical allusions in *Billy Budd*.

Most of chapter 13 (the center of it) was drafted at an early stage (254), as one might suspect from the dominant motif of misconstruing another's motives. (At the time Melville wrote the "coda," such misconstruing was in his mind as the common thread through the whole story up to the end.) Here Claggart, for all his phenomenal qualities, "must have taken" (79) Billy's spilling of his soup for something more than mere accident; and Melville twists the misconstruing further by having Claggart believe the lies about Billy reported by his underling, "Squeak." There is some awkwardness in moving from the third paragraph to the last. The subject is Claggart's misconstruing of Billy, then the third paragraph ends with the warning that Claggart's antipathy is so strong that it does not need to be fed by the lies of his corporal. Melville wrote and then canceled (345) the injunction "Consider." between what now stand as the last word of the third paragraph and the first of the fourth. We might profit by "considering" before reading this opening of the fourth paragraph: "An uncommon prudence is habitual with the subtler depravity, for it has everything to hide" (80). Hating in secret, Claggart may act (against Billy) upon surmise as promptly as upon certainty, and act out of proportion to "the supposed offense" (80). In his analysis of the devious twists in Claggart's thoughts, Melville determines that the self-righteous Pharisee is a subterranean prowler in some natures like Claggart's, natures that "can really form no conception of an unreciprocated malice" (80). The paragraph concludes with the possibility that Claggart's persecution of Billy might have been started to test his qualities and that the soup spilling might have been the first mark he could assign against Billy and might have "put him upon new experiments" (80).

## BILLY AND CLAGGART (CHS. 14-16)

Some form of chapter 16 was written following the composition of chapter 13. In chapter 13, as Hayford and Sealts show, Melville worked out then further expanded "Claggart's use of his corporals to foment trouble for Billy" (254); then in chapter 16 he apparently worked out a passage on Billy's "innocent simplicity" (255). Having thus gotten much of what now stands as chapters 13 and 16 written as a narrative sequence, Melville interpolated the basic content of chapters 14 and 15, writing the new material more fluently because he had already drafted so much of the preceding and following material and knew what he had to tie back to and what he had to link up with. Chapter 14 describes a further and more dangerous stage in the master-at-arms's furtive harassment of Billy Budd through his understrappers, a temptation scene. Billy is "dozing on the uppermost deck," lying "as in the shadow of a hillside, stretched under the lee of the booms" (81), in what a reader (looking back over the story) must take as a foreshadowing of his final night. Still partly unconscious from the deep sleep he had been roused from, he stutters out his anger at the intruder and his threat to "t—t—toss" (82) the fellow over the rail. The passage serves as a classically effective piece of preparation in two other ways: first, caught off guard, Billy cannot explain himself through words. Furthermore, the scene prepares for Billy's insignificant lie at the inquest. Here he does not exactly lie to his friends among the foretopmen—he explains his having stuttered by saying he had found an afterguardsman in his part of the ship, and had run him off. But holding to the code that a man does not tattle, he does not tell his shipmates that he had been approached by someone with what sounded very much like an invitation to join in a mutiny of the impressed men. The sailors in the forecastle "misconstrue" the situation by accepting his partial truth. In his attempt to write a tragedy, although one set down "among the groundlings" (78), Melville adapts the Shakespearean device in which the sense of inevitability is heightened by having a character misconstrue everything. (The phrase I am appropriating here is from *Julius Caesar*, 5.3, spoken by Titinius to the dead Cassius, "Alas, thou hast misconstrued every thing!") In *Billy Budd* several men misconstrue the actions or motives of others, but as often to their credit as to their discredit. In Melville's variation, misconstruing of actions and motives becomes part of the realism of the work: tragedy does not always follow from small misunderstandings, as it does, for instance, in *Othello*.

Chapter 15 is also straightforward, an analysis of Billy's instinctive repugnance to "evil of some sort" (84) and of the direction his curiosity takes him: he wants to see if he can recognize the nocturnal visitor in the daylight, and does, albeit uncertainly. When the afterguardsman responds to Billy's glances with a friendly nod and later an offhand word, Billy is nonplussed. Having no capacity to understand duplicity and no aptitude for detective work, he tries to "smother" the "disturbingly alien" and ineffectual speculations into which he had been led (85). Melville makes clear that the idea of reporting the incident to "the proper quarter" (85) never entered Billy's mind. Had it been suggested, "he would have been deterred from taking it by the thought, one of novice magnanimity, that it would savor overmuch of the dirty work of a telltale" (85). But Billy disburdens himself "a little" to the old Dansker, who rightly concludes, to Billy's astonishment, that it is just as he had warned, "*Jemmy Legs* is *down* on you" (85). The Dansker does not explain himself: "Long experience had very likely brought this old man to that bitter prudence which never interferes in aught and never gives advice" (86).

Chapter 16 begins with what any reader will take as a clear link to the interpolated chapter 15 ("despite the Dansker's pithy insistence," 86), but even that comment may possibly have first been drafted as a reference to the Dansker's earlier "reiteration" of his warning, in chapter 9. Some of the language about Billy's innocence probably survives from a stage when Melville had described the minor harassments of chapter 9 (the "petty trouble" about "such matters as the stowage of his bag or something amiss in his hammock," 68) but had *not* yet written the temptation scene in chapter 14. Beguiled, if not deceived, by the fact that Melville at the start of chapter 16 picks up from the end of chapter 15, no critic has suspected that chapter 16 in its original form picked up from chapter 13 or earlier; even Billy's words about Claggart's always having "a pleasant word" (86) for him go back not to chapters 14 and 15 but chapter 9. The close reader, using the Genetic Text, may well locate further remnants of the earlier function of chapter 16 before the afterguardsman scene was written to precede it.

As it stands, chapter 16 starts with the oddity that "despite" the Dansker's warning Billy cannot believe anything bad of Claggart, who "'always had a pleasant word for him'" (86). This, says Melville, "is to be wondered at. Yet not so much to be wondered at" (86). The "despite" and the "yet" are quickly followed by another word that turns the direction of the thought, a "but" ("But a young seafarer . . . is much of a child-man"). *Another* "yet" follows ("And yet a child's utter innocence"), and still another "but" ("But in Billy Budd") and a third and fourth "yet" ("while yet his simple-mindedness remained" and "yet did Billy's years"); then comes, in almost comical variation, "besides" ("Besides, he had none of that intuitive knowledge of the bad which in natures not good or incompletely so foreruns experience"). The Genetic Text shows that the use of "besides" was an afterthought

(354); Melville had begun the sentence "He" before backing away to offer a further twist. The narrator's vacillations and torturous qualifications mirror Billy's own confusion even while warning us against simple judgments in matters of any psychological complexity, and they also parallel the torturous analysis of Claggart's mind in chapter 13. (Again, before the interpolation of chapters 14 and 15, there may have been an even closer parallel between Claggart's confusing motivations and Billy's confusion.)

The second paragraph (probably drafted after chapters 14 and 15) moves chapter 16 from Billy's special qualities of the "child-man" to the frankness that belongs to seamen in general as opposed to the landsman's finesse, and the third paragraph pushes forward the observation previously focused only on Billy—that "as a class, sailors are in character a juvenile race" (87). Once again Melville moves across time, asserting that his observation was "more especially" true "with the sailors of Billy's time" (87), then (generalizing regardless of time) he contrasts the isolation of the sailor from "promiscuous" (i.e., indiscriminate, random) "commerce with mankind" (a commerce that teaches distrust) with the habitual distrustfulness practiced by landsmen, particularly one class, not businessmen so much as "men who know their kind in less shallow relations than business, namely, certain men of the world" (87). This is a curious construction, for the "namely" seems to point to specific categories, but the categories fade into the vague "certain men of the world." Who are they? In American folklore, Melville knew, men are fitted for certain jobs by their distrust—men who are natural barbers, barkeepers, or salesmen. Or very possibly he had in mind a set of men he had already defined in a passage that was still standing earlier in the story at the time he enlarged this passage—the one on lawyers, experts, clergy which he later discarded. (See the section in Part 4 on "Textual Problems Created by Weaver.")

## MELVILLE BEING HAWTHORNESQUE (CH. 17)

The "core" of chapter 17, Hayford and Sealts show, was drafted early, before chapters 14 and 15 and before a good many elaborations in other chapters that now go before it. In chapter 17 Melville is dealing with a psychological situation which Hawthorne had explored in *The Scarlet Letter*. As we have seen, Hawthorne had been much on Melville's mind, perhaps more after his death in 1864 than in the several years before that when circumstances had kept them from contact with each other. During the long years of writing *Clarel* (1876), Melville had retraced (and rewritten) the psychological history of their friendship, portraying Hawthorne as one of the principal characters, Vine, and he had no doubt come to some peace in doing so (see the "Historical and Critical Note" and the "Historical Supplement" to the Northwestern-Newberry edition). Yet his own loss of his literary career (and fame) and his personal griefs left him extremely vulnerable. Julian Hawthorne as a child had once professed to love Mr. Melville more than anyone except his parents and sister Una, but when he came to see Melville in 1883 as a researcher, Melville (according to Julian's much later report) betrayed his extreme agitation by repeatedly opening and closing a high window with a long pole with a hook at the end (designed to catch a metal eye on the window frame). According to Julian, Melville during this strange performance had offered the opinion that Hawthorne had had some secret in his life which "accounted for the gloomy passages in his books." That is to say, if what Julian recorded is true, that Melville had been reading Hawthorne's life in the light of such works of his as *The Scarlet Letter*, where much is made of "some hideous secret" buried with a man "which he had done better to confess during his lifetime." Hawthorne's fame, cleverly manipulated by his publisher, had soared far past the forgotten Melville's, and even far past the venerated Washington Irving's, and the now-grown Hawthorne children valued the letters they possessed from Melville to Hawthorne not as treasures by the writer of *Moby-Dick* but primarily as contemporary information to help document a period for which their records were oddly thin, the Lenox interlude. Thomas Wentworth Higginson, Emily Dickinson's "tutor," protested in the February 1885 *Atlantic Monthly* (the most prestigious American magazine of the period) against Julian Hawthorne's "'padding'" out *Hawthorne and His Wife* (1885) with "nine consecutive pages of not very interesting epistles from Herman Melville"—the sort of slur which must have been talked about among some members of the Melville family. (A few months after this review appeared, Melville's wife bought *Hawthorne and His Wife* for him, so that he then owned, strangely enough, printed texts of some of his private letters to Hawthorne written at the time of *Moby-Dick*.) Melville had alternated between fascination for Hawthorne the man and for Hawthorne the author; in his later years he seems to have refocused on some of Hawthorne's works. In *Billy Budd* itself, as we have seen, he refers to a character in one of Hawthorne's "minor" (shorter) tales. All this is preliminary to saying that chapter 17 is intensely Hawthornesque.

The situation of chapter 17 is particularly close to one in *The Scarlet Letter*. There Roger Chillingworth insinuates himself into intimate contact (as physician and housemate) with the minister Arthur Dimmesdale. Chillingworth had deceived himself that his "investigation" of Dimmesdale was conducted with the "severe and equal integrity of a judge," but soon he is possessed by "a terrible fascination" and he digs into the minister's heart "like a miner searching for gold" or a sexton "delving into a grave" for a buried jewel. As Chillingworth becomes more evil, the townspeople say that "the fire in his laboratory had been brought from the lower regions, and was fed with infernal fuel; and so, as might be expected, his visage was getting sooty with the smoke." Chillingworth tries to mask his "eager, searching, almost fierce, yet carefully guarded look" with a smile, but the smile plays him false, and flickers "over his visage so derisively, that the spectator could see his blackness all the better for it," and could see now and then "a glare of red light out of his eyes; as if the old man's soul were on fire, and kept on smouldering duskily within his breast." Dimmesdale intuitively shrinks, at times, from the physician, "vaguely aware that something inimical to his peace had thrust itself into relation with him." Intruding once upon his sleeping patient, Chillingworth thrusts aside the garment that covers the minister's chest (in search of some equivalent of the scarlet letter that Hester is sentenced to wear sewn on her clothing) and turns away in a riot of satanic triumph in which, Hawthorne is careful to state, the ecstasy is mingled with a trait of wonder, or awe.

In chapter 17 Claggart secretly watches Billy Budd in mingled emotions, sometimes Christlike ("like the man of sorrows" [88]— a reference to Isaiah 53:3, commonly read by Christians as a prediction of Jesus' fate). Sometimes Claggart looks at Billy with a "soft yearning," as if he "could even have loved Billy but for fate and ban" (88). That last facial expression quickly changes into a pinched look that gives Claggart's face "the momentary semblance of a wrinkled walnut" (88). (Here, the Genetic Text shows [356], Melville had a sentence he later dropped: "Various were these involuntary caprices.") If Claggart sees Billy from a distance and has time to assemble a facial expression, Claggart can regard him "with the glittering dental satire of a Guise" (88), the point being that he might do him some surreptitious wrong in the fashion of a deceitful member of that French ducal house. "But upon any abrupt unforeseen encounter a red light would flash forth from his eye like a spark from an anvil in a dusky smithy" (88). Billy (unlike Dimmesdale) is not instinctively aware of the presence of evil: "the thews of Billy were hardly compatible with that sort of sensitive spiritual organization which in some cases instinctively conveys to ignorant innocence an admonition of the proximity of the malign" (88). The red light is like that flashing from Chillingworth's eyes, and Claggart also Hawthornesquely conceals with a "self-contained and rational demeanor" his monomania in regard to Billy, which "like a subterranean fire, was eating its way deeper and deeper in him" (90).

Melville has worked his way into a characteristically Hawthornesque situation, one appropriate for a subspecies of romance, not for the historical novel that had first seemed to be emerging from his headnote to the ballad. He had offered a justification in chapter 11: the realistic cause of Claggart's antipathy was "in its very realism as much charged with that prime element of Radcliffian romance, the mysterious, as any that the ingenuity of the author of *The Mysteries of Udolpho* could devise" (74). Here, Melville allows for what "shrewd ones may opine" (89) about Billy's failure to go up to the afterguardsman and demand an explanation, and he allows for what else such shrewd ones might think, then concludes that "something more, or rather something else than mere shrewdness is perhaps needful for the due understanding of such a character as Billy Budd's" (90)—or (we recognize) of Claggart's.

THE ACCUSATION (CH. 18)

Hayford and Sealts show that the "first major segment of the manuscript" ends with chapter 17 (256). From chapter 18 through chapter 28, where the death of Vere is reported, the surviving leaves are almost all from very late copying stages. Very little of the matter dealt with in these leaves originated in the early phases of composition. In chapter 18 Claggart's accusation and his confrontation with Billy *is* in fact early-written, and chapters 29 and 30 (the news account and the ballad) are early, but Hayford and Sealts explain that in the long narrative sequence between the confrontation and the news account no leaves from an early stage survive and it must be uncertain just what stood in this sequence in the early stages: "Billy's killing of Claggart was certainly there; and his condemnation, the chaplain's visit, and the hanging must have been reported, but in quite summary fashion" (257). Instead, most of this narrative sequence originated in what they call stage *X,* coming between *D* and *E,* and therefore datable to after November 1888. The actual leaves that survive are from the very late composition-and-copying sequences and bear on them revisions Melville was making up to near the time of his death.

When Melville at the start of chapter 18 turns to "the events now about to be narrated" (90), he is regrouping, expeditiously rehandling some old business (Claggart's interview with Vere) before launching into a new phase of composition. The earlier chapter-opening in the Genetic Text shows the process more baldly: "Some time passed after the abruptly ended interview in the fore-chains" (360). In the opening as we have it, surviving only in late form, Melville reminds the reader that he has already said that Vere's ship was at times employed "on detached service" where "under unforeseen difficulties a prompt initiative might have to be taken in some matter demanding knowledge and ability in addition to those qualities implied in good seamanship" (90). For many readers, this passage sets up the expectation that Vere will possess a degree of personal initiative and courage not unlike that which has already been depicted (in all reading texts) in Nelson. Emphasized in the opening is the danger of the times: the *Bellipotent* has chased a French ship, which has escaped, and Claggart extraordinarily seeks an audience with Vere before the excitement of the sea-chase "had altogether waned away" (91). Vere's reaction to Claggart is Hawthornesque: a "peculiar expression" comes over him "not unlike that which uncontrollably will flit across the countenance of one at unawares encountering a person who, though known to him indeed, has hardly been long enough known for thorough knowledge, but something in whose aspect nevertheless now for the first provokes a vaguely repellent distaste" (91).

When Claggart resorts to circumlocution in alluding to a dangerous character who had "entered His Majesty's service under another form than enlistment," Vere cuts through impatiently: "Be direct, man; say *impressed men*" (92). In the interview which follows, Claggart plays the insinuating, cringing role sometimes adopted by Melville's Babo in "Benito Cereno" and (like Babo's role) derived from Iago's manipulative insinuations and accusations in *Othello*. Here it appears that Vere will be like Othello powerful but unlike Othello insightful and judicious. The focus is on the succession of Vere's feelings, insights, and judgments as Claggart proceeds through his accusatory speeches. Despite his initial annoyance at Claggart's manner and his initial astonishment at the subject Claggart broaches, Vere, by the time the master-at-arms has led up to naming the villain, is ahead of him, already reflecting on the relative merits of two courses—either acting decisively "at the first palpable sign of recurring insubordination" or not being too hasty in crediting the accusation of the informer, since he already recognizes in Claggart (from prior experience) the type of a perjurer (93). (In this story intuitively accurate construing coexists with casual misconstruing.) In the accusation Claggart reminds Vere (94-95) of "that adroit fling of Budd's" on his impressment, the farewell to the *Rights-of-Man* that Vere, and others, had misconstrued as satirical, although he had not judged Billy harshly for what he took as irony. The "misconstruing" theme runs through this crucial passage: these three men are all phenomenal, but Vere does not fully understand Billy's nature. Melville emphasizes that the "something exceptional in the moral quality of Captain Vere" that made him in an interview with another person "a veritable touchstone of that man's essential nature" was now clouded (96). Toward Claggart "and what was really going on in him" Vere did not rely on his "intuitional conviction" as much as "strong suspicion clogged by strange dubieties"—dubieties that had less to do with any faith in Claggart than with practical considerations as to "how best to act in regard to the informer" (96). He represses his first impulse to demand substantiation on the spot, and decides on "a shifting of the scene, a transfer to a place less exposed to observation than the broad quarter-deck" (96-97). The decision is literally a "fatal" one.


## THE CONFRONTATION (CH. 19)

Since "close reading" became the dominant academic approach to any piece of fiction in the 1940s, it has proved almost impossible for anyone to finish reading chapter 19 of *Billy Budd* without wanting to rewrite it. For more than half of the chapter there is no particular problem, although of course there is heightened interest on the part of any reader as Billy is brought to join Captain Vere and Claggart in Vere's cabin. Some of Melville's best late prose is lavished on the depiction of Billy's agony of shock at such an accusation: "Not at first did Billy take it in. When he did, the rose-tan of his cheek looked struck as by white leprosy. He stood like one impaled and gagged" (98). Melville describes Claggart's change of expression (the manuscript shows his struggle to find the right comparison to a fish of the tropics) in language which is characteristically his, not second-rate (or even first-rate) Hawthorne:

> Meanwhile the accuser's eyes, removing not as yet from the blue dilated ones, underwent a phenomenal change, their wonted rich violet color blurring into a muddy purple. Those lights of human intelligence, losing human expression, were gelidly protruding like the alien eyes of certain uncatalogued creatures of the deep. The first mesmeristic glance was one of serpent fascination; the last was as the paralyzing lurch of the torpedo fish. (98)

Vere's encouraging appeal to Billy to speak and defend himself causes "but a strange dumb gesturing and gurgling in Billy" (98). Once again the theme is of intuitive understanding or misconstruing. Here Captain Vere, although ignorant of Billy's vocal impediment, "now immediately divined it" because of a childhood experience in which a schoolmate had been struck by "much the same startling impotence" in an attempt to answer in class (99). Vere's second, and explicitly fatherly, encouragement ends in disaster: although encouraged, Billy still cannot speak, but he can and does strike out. "Fated boy," Vere breathes, "what have you done!" (99). And here the trouble with interpretation begins.

After Vere and Billy together raise the limp Claggart to a sitting position ("It was like handling a dead snake" [99]), Vere undergoes a transformation, covering his face with one hand for a moment then slowly uncovering it: "The father in him, manifested towards Billy thus far in the scene, was replaced by the military disciplinarian" (100). At this point many readers protest that Vere should not have played the father in the first place if he was not going to continue playing the father. Later, after the surgeon has entered and confirmed the death, Vere catches his arm convulsively and exclaims, "It is the divine judgment on Ananias! Look!" (100). The surgeon, disturbed by Vere's "excited manner" (100), holds his peace, then Vere exclaims, "Struck dead by an angel of God! Yet the angel must hang!" (101). Many a reader will protest that Billy is no angel of God but a Handsome Sailor who might not have killed Claggart if Vere had handled the accusation and confrontation in public, and perhaps more customary, manner. The resisting reader also protests at the allusion to the biblical story of Ananias (Acts 5), whom God killed because he lied. Has this captain spent far too much time reading to know how to handle a real ship and real men? The alienated reader may now reevaluate the bookishness that had been presented so favorably in chapter 7 and judge it instead as a sign of moral and intellectual weakness.

In the earlier draft of this passage, Hayford and Sealts explain (9), "the surgeon's part in the scene was purely routine." Vere told the surgeon that the incident could not have happened "at a worse time" (changed to "a time more trying" [376]) either for him or "for the striker of the blow" (9). Hayford and Sealts quote the surgeon's thoughts:

> Too well the thoughtful officer knew what his superior meant. As the former withdrew he could not help thinking how worse than futile the utmost discretion sometimes proves in a world subject to unfor[e]seeable fatalities; the prudent method adopted by Captain Vere to obviate publicity and trouble having resulted in an event that necessitated the former, and, under existing circumstances in the navy indefinit[e]ly magnified the latter. (9)

As Hayford and Sealts say, in these words the surgeon's thoughts "were reported in narrative summary that shaded into authorial commentary" (9).

## THE COURT MARTIAL (CHS. 20-21)

In the earlier draft, what followed chapter 19 was a chapter that began with the manuscript leaves that Weaver mistook as a "preface." The transitional words were the surgeon's thoughts about the "existing circumstances in the navy" (377), and the paragraphs mistaken as the preface were the narrator's meditations on Vere's response to the killing of Claggart. Hayford and Sealts do not print a reading text of this passage, but one can be constructed from their Genetic Text:

> The year 1797, the year of this narrative, belongs to a period which as every thinker now feels, involved a crisis for Christendom not exceeded in its undetermined momentousness at the time by any other era whereof there is record. The opening proposition made by the Spirit of that Age, involved the rectification of the Old World's hereditary wrongs. In France to some extent this was bloodily effected. But what then? Straightway the Revolution regency as righter of wrongs itself became a wrongdoer, one more oppressive than the Kings. Under Napoleon it enthroned upstart kings, and initiated that prolonged agony of Continental war whose final throes was at Waterloo. During those years not the wisest could have for[e]seen that the outcome of all would be what to some thinkers since out to be [Melville meant the sense to be something like "has since turned out to be"], a political advance along nearly the whole line for Europeans.
>
> Now as elsewhere hinted, it was something caught from the Revolutionary Spirit that at Spithead emboldened the man-of-war's men to rise against real abuses, long-standing ones, and afterwards at the Nore to make inordinate and aggressive demands, successful resistance to which was confirmed only when the ringleaders were hung for an admonitory spectacle to the anchored fleet. Yet in a way analagous [analogous] to the operation of the Revolution at large the Great Mutiny, tho' by Englishmen naturally deemed monstrous at the time, doubtless gave the first latent prompting to most important reforms in the British navy. (377-78)

As Hayford and Sealts say, it was "on the basis of these reflections that the narrator then in effect underwrote Vere's view of the case, doing so in the course of an extended passage still standing in the final manuscript" (10), the one which concludes with the paragraph beginning "Feeling that unless quick action was taken" (ch. 21, 104). So as Melville first wrote the passage any tendency a reader might have to resist the account of Vere's behavior was checked, if not altogether dismissed, by the narrator's lengthy reflections on the circumstances which made the time the most dangerous for the ship and the most luckless for Billy.

What Melville did to the manuscript at this point must again be summarized from Hayford and Sealts (10-11). For six leaves of the manuscript (including what Weaver mistook as the "preface") Melville substituted eight leaves emphasizing Vere's agitation and the fact that the surgeon is "profoundly discomposed" by Vere's "passionate interjections" as well as "disturbed" by Vere's "desire for secrecy" (10). Rather than guiding us to support Vere by means of the passage on the Revolutionary Spirit, Melville in the revision does something quite contrary to that—he elaborates on the surgeon's "disquietude" and the startling new question as to whether Vere "was suddenly affected in his mind" (11). The surgeon now questions the propriety of a drumhead court, and the officers are said to agree with him that Billy's fate had better be left till the ship has rejoined the squadron, where the case could be referred to the admiral. Hayford and Sealts sum up the situation:

> Finally, in two paragraphs that serve as a new introduction to the next chapter (Ch. 21), Melville pushed even further the question of Vere's state of mind, asking as narrator: "Who in the rainbow can draw the line" between sanity and insanity? And he concludes, noncommittally: "Whether Captain Vere, as the Surgeon professionally & privately surmised, was really the sudden victim of any degree of aberration, every one must determine for himself by such light as this narrative may afford." (11)

As they say, it is "by no means clear" (11) what answer Melville expected the reader to arrive at.

As Melville left chapters 19 and 20 at his latest revisions, the change of Vere from father to military disciplinarian is almost at once followed by the entrance of the "self-poised" surgeon. We learn very quickly that the surgeon regards as disturbing Vere's postures, or posturings (he stands motionless, at one point, "with one hand to his brow" [100]). Thus far, the reader has every reason to feel that this sensible surgeon is the one to be trusted. To be sure, the surgeon is to some extent undercut by Melville's questions at the beginning of chapter 21, for these questions of the line between sanity and insanity are questions such as in any era men and women will take good money for answering: "There is nothing namable but that some men will, or undertake to, do it for pay" (102). Melville cannot edge close to the topic of what we would call "expert witnesses" without feeling some of the anger that went into the long-since excised "Lawyers, Experts, Clergy" (338; see the discussion of ch. 12, p. 122 above). But at this point the surgeon is not explicitly challenged.

In the story as it stands, the surgeon's astonishment at Vere's decision to convene a court martial at once rather than to wait and to refer such a matter "to the admiral" is said (at the end of chapter 20) to have been "fully shared" by "the lieutenants and captain of marines" (102), ample evidence that his opinion is not peculiar in any way, and his suspicions as to Vere's sanity are apparently substantiated by the narrator's eloquent rhetorical question which begins chapter 21. But these passages are followed in the text by earlier-written narratorial commentary which seems to support Vere. "Small wonder" (103) Vere acted as he did. He may have erred, the narrator concedes, and he was later "not a little criticized by some officers" on other ships, and the secrecy in which Vere conducted the whole proceedings was ground for "invidious comment" (103). Melville even says that Vere would have preferred to withhold action until the ship rejoined the squadron, but he was "a true military officer" with a monklike adherence to his "martial duty" (104). Vere, in other words, thought he had no choice. It is not explained why other officers in other ships, as well as officers on his own ship, thought that he did have such an option and indeed that it might have been better to exercise it, and let the admiral make the final decision on Billy Budd. After Vere's behavior and indeed his sanity have been called into question, the text continues with the paragraph that originally followed what Weaver mistook as a "preface":

> Feeling that unless quick action was taken on it, the deed of
> the foretopman, so soon as it should be known on the gun decks,
> would tend to awaken any slumbering embers of the Nore

among the crew, a sense of the urgency of the case overruled in Captain Vere every other consideration. But though a conscientious disciplinarian, he was no lover of authority for mere authority's sake. Very far was he from embracing opportunities for monopolizing to himself the perils of moral responsibility, none at least that could properly be referred to an official superior or shared with him by his official equals or even subordinates. So thinking, he was glad it would not be at variance with usage to turn the matter over to a summary court of his own officers, reserving to himself . . . the right of maintaining a supervision of it, or formally or informally interposing at need. (104)

The narrator's statement remains: Vere's understanding of military law is that his procedure is not at variance with usage. Melville here makes no suggestion that Vere was misinformed. Again, this section was written *before* a section that now stands ahead of it, the surgeon's thought that it would be more politic to wait until the ship had rejoined the squadron.

Did Melville mean the surgeon's knowledge of military usage to be conspicuously defective, and to be corrected here? Hardly: Melville was not setting the surgeon up for quick straightening out on legal procedure. We are stuck with a text which is confused on precisely a point where we strongly want to know what the facts are. Some readers, understandably, have tried to determine what British naval usage really was in 1797, but having an accurate report of legal opinions of the time would do us no good, since Melville himself plainly was not sure and did not make (did not take the time to make or did not have the strength to make) sufficient effort to find out, and in any case, having had lawyers in the family he knew that the law is always subject to interpretation. As heirs of the New Critics, we find it hard to accept the fact that some contradictions in literary works are not deliberate, not planted there as challenges to our ingenuity which delights in plucking higher unity out of apparent discrepancy. Even if we could establish the precise historical status of naval law we would not be better off; however much we dislike unintentional and uncontrolled ambivalence, we are left with a story in which there are two contrary versions of what the law was, and we must live without an indication from the author that one version is right and the other is wrong.

It seems to many readers that the court martial scene in chapter 21 goes very far to demonstrate why some of Vere's contemporaries thought that a "pedantic" (63) streak showed in his behavior and also that the scene goes far to undermine Melville's earlier efforts to depict Vere as a phenomenal man. If he is a phenomenal man, why does he act as if he had no possible choice? Melville's concern throughout the court martial scene needs to be paid particular attention because almost all readers tend to push their own ideological demands into the text here. Melville portrays Vere as "sinking his rank" so he can testify, but retaining control through the "apparently trivial" means of standing higher than the members of the court, who are on the lee side (105). He manifests his official power by seizing the position of physical advantage. Billy's replies to the court's questions twice evoke from Vere the declaration that he believes Billy, and on the one occasion when Billy temporizes, unable to inform on the afterguardsman now any more than he could inform on him at the time of the hurried temptation, and then finally (it may be said) tells a lie, the response of everyone in the room is to believe him. The seriousness of the failure to inform on a shipmate does not weigh anything in Billy's scale of values, and apparently not in Melville's. It is Billy's "erring sense of uninstructed honor" (106) which keeps him silent, and the "erring" seems almost inconsequential to the narrator. When the officer of marines asks Billy why Claggart should have lied, Billy is nonplussed, and turns "an appealing glance towards Captain Vere as deeming him his best helper and friend" (107). Vere rises again, taking again a position above the officers of the court, and directs attention to the consequence of Billy's blow, not to Claggart's motivation. (As several times before, Melville uses animal imagery of Billy, comparing his appealing look toward Vere to that of "a dog of generous breed" [107].)

Billy apparently does not understand the import of what Vere has said, but the members of the court recognize "a prejudgment on the speaker's part" (108). The next sentence is "It served to augment a mental disturbance previously evident enough." The Genetic Text does not offer any help here on the question of whose mental disturbance has been previously evident and is now augmented. Not Billy's, who would not fully have caught the unanticipated meaning involving a prejudgment on Vere's part. Vere's

words would not have served to augment his own mental disturbance (although because Vere's sanity has already been called into
question one may first want to associate these words with him).
Presumably it is the members of the court who have already been
mentally disturbed by the events (including the testimony), and
who have just felt a "marked effect" (108) from Vere's words.
Vere's utterance made their mental distress more severe.

Vere then pushes the court away from further inquiry, himself
using the scriptural phrase "mystery of iniquity," but insisting that
a military court has nothing to do with such complexities (108).
Vere by a glance retakes the primacy in the court from the first
lieutenant. After Billy is led out, the three officers stir in their
seats and exchange "looks of troubled indecision" (109), but Captain Vere takes another powerful physical position—standing with
his back toward them—then unconsciously climbs "the slant deck
in the ship's lee roll," symbolizing "a mind resolute to surmount
difficulties even if against primitive instincts strong as the wind
and the sea" (109). The narrator reports, without judgment, that
Vere seemed to regard the officers as "well-meaning men not intellectually mature" (109), to whom things obvious to him would
have to be demonstrated. Vere cannot modify his learned phraseology to fit the simpler minds of his officers, and he cannot try to
hide the pedantic streak alleged against him by less-bookish and
more practical captains. Melville gives the gist of his comments
(110): an insistence that "natural justice" is not at consideration;
sailors are not "natural free agents"; they "fight at command,"
whether or not they approve the war:

> For suppose condemnation to follow these present proceedings.
> Would it be so much we ourselves that would condemn as it
> would be martial law operating through us? For that law and the
> rigor of it, we are not responsible. (110-11)

When it is clear that his arguments are agitating the three men
but not convincing them, Vere "abruptly" changes his tone and
directs their attention to the fact that the blow was a capital crime
"according to the Articles of War" (111). The officer of marines
"emotionally" breaks in to say that Billy purposed neither mutiny
nor homicide. In his quick reply Vere pounces (can we fairly say?)
on a pedantic distinction:

> "Surely not, my good man. And before a court less arbitrary
> and more merciful than a martial one, that plea would largely
> extenuate. At the Last Assizes it shall acquit. But how here? We
> proceed under the law of the Mutiny Act." (111)

In what follows Vere plays upon the sense of urgency, reproaching
members of the court for the amount of time they are taking
("while thus strangely we prolong proceedings that should be summary" [112]) when the enemy may at any moment be sighted. He
offers an option that he had conspicuously not offered before: "one
of two things must we do—condemn or let go" (112).

Just before this, in depicting Vere in the process of choosing
his words carefully so his intellectually inferior officers can comprehend him, Melville gave no clue as to his own tone toward that
manipulative condescension. Now Vere speculates with his inferior
officers about how to deal with a yet more inferior group:

> "The people" (meaning the ship's company) "have native sense;
> most of them are familiar with our naval usage and tradition;
> and how would they take it [freeing Billy]? Even could you ex-
> plain to them—which our official position forbids—they, long
> molded by arbitrary discipline, have not that kind of intelligent
> responsiveness that might qualify them to comprehend and dis-
> criminate." (112)

The crew, Vere insists, would take a merciful sentence as pusillani-
mous: "They would think that we flinch, that we are afraid of
them—afraid of practicing a lawful rigor singularly demanded at
this juncture, lest it should provoke new troubles" (113).

Melville makes it clear that the members of the court, as loyal
lieges, "hardly had the inclination, to gainsay one whom they felt
to be an earnest man, one too not less their superior in mind than
in naval rank" (113). But Melville also stresses that Vere had appealed "to their instinct as sea officers" (113) to dread the consequences if the killing were not promptly punished. Here Melville
cites the execution of three men as mutineers on the U.S. brig-of-
war *Somers* in 1842, in peacetime. Although he was in the Pacific
when the episode occurred, he had learned a great deal about it,
for it was over the course of many months a major news story and
his own first cousin Guert Gansevoort (who as the oldest male in
the line inherited the medal of the Cincinnati that belonged to

their grandfather, the "Hero of Fort Stanwix," Peter Gansevoort)
was one of the officers responsible for the executions. (Decisively
damaged by the event, Guert declined into ill health, alcoholism,
loss of naval commands, and too-early death.) Melville cites the
*Somers* case without comment, he says, but actually he draws a
parallel: "the urgency felt, well-warranted or otherwise" (114), was
much the same as on the *Bellipotent*.

If a reader has been protesting against the chapter, paragraph
by paragraph, looking for evidence that Vere is being covertly criticized for his assurance of intellectual and moral superiority, then
the next paragraph dashes that expectant mood. Melville quotes
"a writer whom few know" (Melville himself, observe Hayford and
Sealts [34]) for the reflection that "Forty years after a battle it is
easy for a noncombatant to reason about how it ought to have been
fought" (114). The reader who criticizes Vere is implicitly compared to "the snug card players in the [passenger] cabin" who
little think "of the responsibilities of the sleepless man on the
bridge." This paragraph controls our response to the next, which
announces that "Billy Budd was formally convicted and sentenced
to be hung at the yardarm in the early morning watch" (114).

## THE PRIVATE MEETING OF BILLY AND CAPTAIN VERE (CH. 22)

The body of chapter 22, where Vere sees Billy alone to tell him
of the decision of the court, is reported with remarkable indirect-
ness. The narrator does not tell what happened but what "would
have been in consonance with the spirit of Captain Vere" to do,
even to telling Billy frankly of his own part in bringing about the
decision (115). As for Billy, "it is not improbable that such a confession would have been received in much the same spirit that
prompted it" (115). The only undeniable fact about the interview
is that during it Vere told Billy that he was to be hanged in the
morning. The narrator ventures "some conjectures" (115) in view
"of the character of the twain briefly closeted in that stateroom,
each radically sharing in the rarer qualities of our nature—so rare
indeed as to be all but incredible to average minds however much
cultivated" (114-15). Here the narrator seems to underwrite Vere's
sense of his own intellectual superiority, and the passage flatly
asserts the rare qualities of the nature of both Billy and Vere. The

reader may have looked through chapter 21 in vain for evidence that Vere is what we had been told he was, a phenomenal man, but the narrator in this passage (written before the part where the surgeon wonders whether or not Vere is insane and the narrator asks who can draw the line between sanity and insanity) admits no doubt on that score.

For many readers the problem with this chapter is that the depiction of Vere as a phenomenal man, one of "great Nature's nobler order" (115) has been undercut by the surgeon's perturbed thoughts in chapter 20 and by Vere's rigid, unimaginative role in chapter 21, where he rejects the claims of Nature (110) by insisting that he sailed under the Articles of War (111): now in chapter 22 the man who has just rejected the claims of Nature is oddly honored as one of great Nature's noblemen. Chapters 20 and 21 together subvert the attitude toward Vere that Melville seems to want the reader to take in chapter 22.

In his early writings Melville tended to exalt absolute commitment to an idealistic goal above timid reliance on conventional practices. Several of his early characters imitate the absolute behavior of Jesus only to come to grief in the practical, relativistic world. Melville used the device of an interpolated philosophical pamphlet in *Pierre* to oppose idealistic, "chronometrical" behavior (perhaps suitable for use in heaven) against expedient, "horological" behavior such as this world expects and rewards. Melville's attraction to idealistic rather than legalistic behavior continued into the time of his work on *Billy Budd*. A reader of "Bridegroom-Dick" in Melville's *John Marr* (1888) would be predisposed to expect phenomenal behavior from Vere. There Captain Turret must deal with a favorite seaman of his, the Finn who has drunk himself into a berserk fit. Putting on his "martinet-mien," in which facial expression one may see written the Articles of War, Captain Turret has the Finn strapped up for scourging, since discipline "must be." Then the magnanimous Turret orders that the Finn be untied: "Flog? Never meant it—hadn't any heart. / Degrade that tall fellow?" The implicit answer is "no," and nautical discipline does not suffer because of such magnanimity. Readers familiar with attitudes Melville expressed elsewhere sometimes argue that he is ironic here in chapter 22 of *Billy Budd*, but there is nothing in the surviving text to support a reading of chapter 21 as an exposé of

Vere's conventionalism as contrasted, say, to Nelson's greater heroism. Melville in chapter 22 treats Vere with deep respect. Anyone unhappy with what goes on in chapter 21 and chapter 22 should not look for a clue to an overall pattern of interpretation which will clarify all that is inconsistent in Vere's character. And one should not look for a literary theory that will assure him or her that art should be like life, inconsistent. Rather, the reader should force himself or herself to look section by section, or sometimes scene by scene, at what role Melville had for Vere at *this* point and *that* point. And always there is the problem for the reader, as there was for Melville himself, of what to do with the Nelson pages.

When Melville was drafting chapters 21 and 22, where was the Nelson chapter? At stage *Da* (from November to December 1888?), Hayford and Sealts say, Melville decided to exclude the Nelson chapter, and at this time "he withdrew it from the sequence and placed it in a separate folder" (245). At stage *Eb* he seems to have had second thoughts, but he did not restore it to the manuscript; he did, however, leave a gap for it in his numbering so that he could slip it in if he decided to. At *G* he apparently resolved "on its restoration" (246), and revised and recopied some of the leaves. At this stage he added the opening comments about the "literary sin" he was committing (303). Still hesitant, he numbered the pages of the new Nelson sequence one through ten but did not insert them into the manuscript and did not assign them the *E* numbers he had reserved (51-59). Hayford and Sealts show exactly what he did: he "passed on to revise the scene between Vere and the surgeon. That he did revise that scene shortly after revising the Nelson chapter is indicated by his use of the verso" of a superseded Nelson leaf for writing part of "the revised Vere-surgeon scene" (246). Hayford and Sealts assume, as Weaver had done, that Melville's intention was to restore the Nelson chapter, since he was revising it in the very latest stages he worked on the manuscript.

However, the fact that Melville did not restore the Nelson chapter despite many opportunities to do so may indicate a profound ambivalence. Melville knew that the chapter was wonderful, but something about it seems to have perturbed him. Melville had gone far past the point where being accused of digressing would have upset him very much. Chances are that he saw, every time he

looked at the leaves in the separate folder, that if he put that
chapter back in the manuscript no reader could fail to hold Nelson
up as a standard against which Vere would be judged, and that
any comparison between the two would be in Nelson's favor, so
that the reader would be predisposed to resist any support the
narrator might give to Vere after the killing of Claggart.

While some Melville critics protest against chapter 22 as un-
believable after what has occurred in the two previous chapters,
others explain it as an archetypal reconciliation fantasy. And in the
simplest descriptive terms the chapter is a speculation so bold and
so personal as to be all but indistinguishable from fantasy, since
there are said to be no witnesses to what is depicted and all we
know of it is what the narrator imagines would have been conso-
nant with the spirit of Vere (and of Billy). Indeed, Melville gives a
hint to any psychologic theologians among his readers when he
compares Vere's seizing Billy to his heart (*if* of course Vere actually
did embrace Billy at the end of the interview—something we do
not know) to Abraham's possibly catching young Isaac to him
before (not after) he began the sacrifice. There is no embrace in
Genesis 22, of course, and only a ram is sacrificed, as it turns out,
not Isaac: God is only testing Abraham's obedience, and Vere is
determined to hang Billy. Melville's image is of father willing to
sacrifice a son, but also of reconciliation between father and son.
Vere does not feel himself a prodigal father (to judge by what we
learn of his remorse-free death); and Billy has hardly been a prodigal son. In any case, there is no joyous reconciliation, with fatted
calf killed and feasted upon. If the embrace occurred, it had no
overt consequences.

Melville had himself suffered grievous losses without such a
therapeutic reconciliation scene. When he was twelve and a half
his father died after a sickness in which his mind wandered, to put
the mildest construction on the contemporary testimony: we can be
sure there never occurred an earnest deathbed scene in which Allan
Melvill singled out the third child of his brood of eight for an
embrace healing enough to send him unscathed through the ago-
nies of the coming decades. When Melville was twenty-six his older
brother Gansevoort (who had just succeeded in having *Typee* published for him) died alone in London; slowness of communication
meant that Melville wrote Gansevoort a hearty letter after the

destined recipient was dead. There was no "completing" (to use our jargon) of that relationship either, and in *Timoleon* (put into shape during the composition of *Billy Budd*) Melville returned to the powerful and obviously unresolved topic of sibling rivalry, a topic as fresh and painful to great old artists as to any slighted child.

While we can never say what figures loom largest in someone else's imagination as unreconciled with, or as representing an "uncompleted" relationship, we can acknowledge that it would not have been against nature if Allan Melvill and Gansevoort Melville were for all Herman Melville's life his two most important male relatives, the two exerting most power in his conscious or unconscious states decades after they were dead. The living presence of the dead in the Melvilles' lives comes home when we consider that Melville's sister Fanny gave their nephew Frank Hoadley on his eleventh birthday in 1876 a letter their mother (dead since 1872) had written in 1826, half a century before, about the academic triumphs of her oldest son, Gansevoort; Fanny endorsed the letter: "Given to Frank . . . in remembrance of his Uncle Gansevoort"— an uncle who died nineteen years before Frank was born. But Melville had been a friend in early life to many men, including Jack Chase and Nathaniel Hawthorne (both of whom were powerfully on his mind as he wrote *Billy Budd*), the only two men outside his family to whom he dedicated works of fiction, *Moby-Dick* to Hawthorne, *Billy Budd* to Chase. Did he still need a reconciliation with either? And Melville had been a father of two sons as well as a son and brother, and his sons were both dead, one in 1867, the other early in 1886, about the time he began reworking the headnote to "Billy in the Darbies." There was no reconciliation scene with either. The Melville household had been miserable for years before 1867—so much so that not only Elizabeth Shaw Melville's relatives but also at least some of the Melvilles agreed that Herman Melville was insane and were ready to shelter her if she decided to separate from him, so miserable that her minister proposed a fantastic and utterly illegal scheme for her to take refuge with her brothers in Boston. Instead, Melville's wife stayed with him, and a few months later Melville harshly imposed a curfew on his eighteen-year-old son Malcolm, and the boy whose birth had been so promising and whose teens had been so sad shot himself to death in his bed, not to be discovered until his father came home from work and broke open the door. Melville weirdly wrote to his brother-in-law John Hoadley that Malcolm had never said an unfilial word to him in his life. Malcolm, of course, as the thanatologist Edwin S. Shneidman thinks, had just committed the ultimately unfilial act. (For all we know Malcolm, barely post-adolescent, saw himself as his mother's knight and killed himself when it became quite clear that he could do nothing more than his Shaw uncles to help a suffering woman who refused to cooperate with her would-be rescuers.) And the second son, conceived while Melville was enthralled with the composition of *Moby-Dick* and born the month it was published in London as *The Whale*, had a happy and successful father for about six weeks of his life, before the reviews of *Moby-Dick* began appearing. Untrained, apparently unapt for specialized training of any sort, Stanwix drifted—across Central America, across the United States (Indian Territory, Kansas, terrain his wandering father never trod), until he died in San Francisco. Melville was not there to clasp him to his bosom.

In view of such unresolved relationships, it may well be that reconciliation fantasy colors the passage describing the unwitnessed scene between Vere and Billy:

> But there is no telling the sacrament, seldom if in any case revealed to the gadding world, wherever under circumstances at all akin to those here attempted to be set forth two of great Nature's nobler order embrace. There is privacy at the time, inviolable to the survivor; and holy oblivion, the sequel to each diviner magnanimity, providentially covers all at last. (115)

Vere, seen leaving the compartment, bears an expression "of the agony of the strong" (115). Vere, it is hinted, suffered more than Billy did, and in the last line of the chapter Melville looks forward to the death words of Vere, which will go far to prove that the captain suffered more than the Handsome Sailor he hanged.

## BILLY'S LAST NIGHT (CHS. 23-24)

In chapter 23 there is no discussion of what might have occurred. Instead, all is straightforward. The narrator at the outset acknowledges that incidents can come so rapidly that recounting them can take longer in the telling than the events did in the happening, especially if the teller feels "explanation or comment" seem required: less than an hour and a half elapsed between Claggart's entering Vere's cabin and the interview between Vere and Billy Budd (116). In this time, the narrator tells us, rumors spread through the ship that something was going on involving Claggart and Billy, "the people of a great warship being in one respect like villagers, taking microscopic note of every outward movement or non-movement going on" (116). The crew, then, is "not wholly unprepared" for some announcement when all hands are called to deck in the second dogwatch, between six and eight in the evening (116). Melville makes absolutely no romance of the setting:

> There was a moderate sea at the time; and the moon, newly risen and near to being at its full, silvered the white spar deck wherever not blotted by the clear-cut shadows horizontally thrown of fixtures and moving men. On either side the quarterdeck the marine guard under arms was drawn up; and Captain Vere, standing in his place surrounded by all the wardroom officers, addressed his men. (116)

Vere announces clearly and concisely what has taken place, concluding with the information that Billy would be executed "in the early morning watch" (117). There is no gothic gloom here, no fitful swaying of shadows, no full light of moon falling upon the agonized face of the captain. Vere does not *look* as if anything out of the ordinary has occurred, and nature is going about its own business. The man in the moon does not take part in the action; there are, in short, no lurid effects such as Hawthorne relied upon in "My Kinsman, Major Molineux."

Two long paragraphs are devoted to rigorously controlled narration of Vere's rigorously staged announcement, then the short third paragraph contains a simile which hurls the reader's mind out of the black and white moonlight scene into another dark scene:

> Their captain's announcement was listened to by the throng of standing sailors in a dumbness like that of a seated congregation of believers in hell listening to the clergyman's announcement of his Calvinistic text. (117)

("Believers in hell" means believers in the existence of hell, not believers who are now in hell; a note Melville made in the manuscript suggests, as Hayford and Sealts say, that he "may have intended to work in an allusion to Jonathan Edwards" [264].) The paragraph stresses a grim fatalism where direst expectation is matched by the actual announcement of captain or clergyman. Therefore the next paragraph, also short, is startling in its description of the "confused murmur" that went up at the end of Vere's words—at the naming of the time for Billy's execution (117). The murmur is suppressed by "shrill whistles," and all goes in orderly fashion, including the burial of Claggart, which is tersely told, so as "not to clog the sequel with lateral matters" (117). The tone reverts to that of the first two paragraphs as the narrator records the "strict adherence to usage" that prevailed, making it clear that man-of-war's men were "of all men the greatest sticklers for usage" (117). Just as the sound of the boatswain's and his mates' whistles broke up the confused murmur, so adherence to usage reassures the men and controls them. Having ended the chapter with the words "vigilance may be augmented" (118), Melville added two more sentences, in the same tone, preparing for the chaplain's visit to Billy.

Hayford and Sealts show that some of the material of chapter 24 must have been part of the very earliest stages of the story, since it elaborates the chaplain's visit, which was part of the ballad. Perhaps because the matter if not the final wording of much of chapter 24 dates from so early a stage, the tone differs from that of the several preceding chapters. Here the narrator displays Billy to view, commanding the reader to "behold" him "under sentry lying prone in irons in one of the bays formed by the regular spacing of the guns comprising the batteries on either side" (118). (Hayford and Sealts suggest [265] that the parts of the second and third paragraphs describing Billy in the present tense may have been drafted as part of the headnote, before *Billy Budd* became a "story.")

The second paragraph (118-19) contains some remarkable onomatopoetic and alliterative reminders of the weight, massiveness, and inertia of the now-antiquated guns near which Billy is chained. The guns are mounted on *lumbering* wooden carriages, they are *hampered* with *cumbersome* "harness of breeching and strong side-tackles" for *running them out*. Long *rammers* and shorter linstocks are "lodged in loops overhead." Guns, carriages, rammers, linstocks are all, "as customary," painted black, and "the heavy *hempen* breechings, tarred to the same tint, wore the like livery of the undertakers." In contrast to this blackness and massiveness and weight and resistance to movement, Billy lies in his jumper and white duck trousers, somewhat soiled from wear so that his clothing "dimly glimmered in the obscure light of the bay like a patch of discolored snow in early April lingering at some upland cave's black mouth." The battle lanterns, fed with foul oil bought from war contractors, "pollute the pale moonshine," and other lanterns cast enough light to make the "obscurer bays" look like small confessionals or side-chapels in a cathedral. Nothing in the passage makes a judgment on this comparison—there is no ironic comparison, no playing on similarities between a place devoted to the worship of God and a place devoted to pursuit of war. The comparison is left at the level of visual similarity.

Avoiding melodrama in a situation which invites gothicizing (something on the level of "during the few fleeting hours pallor had gnawed like nitre through the rose-tan of the sailor's face, fast exposing the skeleton beneath"), Melville takes a realistic view of how long imprisonment would have to last before Billy would have paled. Yet he achieves a heightened, subtler form of psychological effect than was common in the gothic novels such as *The Mysteries of Udolpho* (referred to in ch. 11): "the skeleton in the cheekbone at the point of its angle was just beginning delicately to be defined under the warm-tinted skin" (119). The reason Billy's flesh begins to waste is that he (like Mortmain, one of the characters in *Clarel*) has a fervid heart "self-contained," the kind of heart in which "some brief experiences devour our human tissue as secret fire in a ship's hold consumes cotton in the bale" (119). Melville says *our* "human tissue"; in his decades of shame and obscurity he knew all there was to know about "fervid hearts self-contained" (119).

The fourth paragraph (119-20) offers factual information which the reader may or may not find consoling; and the narrator does not *push* its consoling value. We could have guessed that Billy's agony proceeded mainly "from a generous young heart's virgin experience of the diabolical[,] incarnate and effective in some men" but it is news to us that the "tension" of his agony is over: "It survived not the something healing in the closeted interview with Captain Vere." Now Billy lies as in a trance, his expression something like that of "a slumbering child in the cradle" at night as the lingering "hearth-glow" touches dimples that form and unform in its cheek. The comparison is disturbing, partly because we remember that Billy was a foundling (and because we know almost nothing about what care he himself received in the cradle), partly for other reasons, such as Billy's present vulnerability.

During the course of working on the story, Melville expanded his first version of this chapter then cut it back down a little by removing a leaf which apparently elaborated his reflections on the anomaly of having a chaplain on board a man-of-war. One of the recurrent themes of his early works was the failure of Christians to behave like Christ, and for Melville to think of a chaplain enlisted in the military was to feel both satirical amusement and the pain of a tragic lesson in the impracticability of Christianity. In the fundamentalist view of Christianity which infused him (despite some fundamentalists' denunciations of his works as blasphemous), Melville saw that a chaplain on a warship could not possibly do his duty as a servant of God: his pay came from the military. Specifically, what Melville revealed in some of his early works was a sense of intense longing to believe that absolute obedience to the words of Jesus was possible and a sense (felt simultaneously or almost so) that from any attempt at the absolute imitation of Jesus what could come was either tragic sacrifice or ignoble compromise. He could satirize the nominal practice of Christianity while still agonizing over the knowledge that Christianity was, as far as he could see, impracticable in this world.

In characterizing the chaplain in chapter 24 Melville restrained both his idealistic impulses and his satiric impulses. The irony is inescapable (the "minister of Christ" receives "his stipend from Mars" [120]) but not sharpened or twisted. The minister himself, although compromised by the very fact of his being on a man-of-war, is not otherwise hypocritical. The first time he comes near to Billy he moves delicately away, and when he comes back he does not insist on "his vocation," deciding, against that calling, that "innocence was even a better thing than religion wherewith to go to Judgment" (121). Although in chapter 22 Melville denied us the interview between Billy and Vere, here he offers a "strange" scene which is also healing. The chaplain withdraws only after "performing an act strange enough in an Englishman, and under the circumstances yet more so in any regular priest" (121). He "kissed on the fair cheek his fellow man, a felon in martial law, one whom though on the confines of death he felt he could never convert to a dogma; nor for all that did he fear for his future" (121). In the interview with Captain Vere there had been something healing for Billy; now at least the man whose job is to admonish and console may himself be consoled.

Again Melville addresses the reader: "Marvel not"—marvel not that the chaplain "lifted not a finger to avert the doom of such a martyr to martial discipline" (121). "Bluntly put," and Melville is blunt enough, "a chaplain is the minister of the Prince of Peace serving in the host of the God of War—Mars" (122). In Melville's tone there is no rejoicing (no glee at delivering news which must be unwelcome to novice readers), no reformer's zeal (no attempt to incite the reader to *change* things), but merely a cool sense of the way things are: in this world the religion of peace serves "brute Force."

Throughout chapter 24, as in the early chapters, the narrator stresses how things were at times in the past—what the upper gundeck was like in a seventy-four-cannon battleship "of the old order" (118); the heaviness of the caliber of the cannons "of that period" (118); the foulness of the oil supplied by the war contractors of 1797 (with a glance at the war contractors whose gains in any war are "an anticipated portion of the harvest of death" [119]). Furthermore, he stresses the similarity of Billy as "barbarian" to "the British captives, living trophies, made to march in the Roman triumph of Germanicus" (120); then Billy's similarity as barbarian to the later British converts to Christianity (or nominal converts) taken to Rome. Here Melville's mind leaps to compare those British converts with present-day "converts from lesser isles of the sea" (120—"East Indian," he specified in a deleted phrase [407]) who may be taken to London, not to Rome; then, instead of recalling Billy again, Melville compares the later British converts of the Dark Ages to painted figures still later "in time," in the Renaissance, Fra Angelico's angels (121). In the next paragraph Billy as pagan is compared to a South Sea islander of "long ago," then more specifically to "a Tahitian, say, of Captain Cook's time or shortly after that time" (121). Here Melville's imagination is minutely historical, for he works in shadings, the difference not between eighteenth century and nineteenth century but between the time Captain Cook encounters "so-called" (120) savages utterly innocent of Christianity and the time only a little later when the corruption of the natives had begun, long before Melville's own time in the South Seas, when in Tahiti Christianity had usurped the traditional religion and when European diseases (venereal and otherwise) were pushing the Polynesians toward annihilation—when Paradise was becoming a sewer. These paragraphs demand that we as readers of *Billy Budd* attempt to hold in our own memories something of Melville's thick, thronging, chronologically and geographically vast sense of world history in which his decades of both random and purposeful reading is inextricably fused with his extraordinary early personal experiences and his decades of reflections upon those experiences.

The movement of the sixth paragraph deserves special attention for its oddity. It begins with an explanation of how Billy could rest, unafraid of death:

> Not that like children Billy was incapable of conceiving what death really is. No, but he was wholly without irrational fear of it, a fear more prevalent in highly civilized communities than those so-called barbarous ones which in all respects stand nearer to unadulterate Nature. (120)

(Hayford and Sealts do not establish whether this part of chapter 24 preceded or followed the inscription of Vere's words on Nature at the court martial [261, 264].) In his British barbarism Billy is first compared to barbaric British captives displayed in Rome by Germanicus, then to the hardly less barbaric British converts to Christianity in a later century. Then Billy as the point of comparison is almost wholly lost, and the angelic looking Angles he was compared to usurp primacy, and *they* (not Billy) are compared to angels painted in the Italian Renaissance by a painter with a seraphic name, Fra Angelico, some of whose angels, "plucking apples in gardens of the Hesperides, have the faint rosebud complexion of the more beautiful English girls," not boys like Billy (121). Instead, Billy is left far back in the paragraph, last tied to the barbaric nominal converts. Is the movement of this paragraph akin to the movement of parts of the first two chapters, particularly the "nautical Murat" and "Billy-be-Dam" section of chapter 1? Has

Melville at this point lost control or else never asserted control over the paragraph? Is a sort of unconscious avoidance-fantasy leading Melville so far away from Billy?

## THE HANGING (CH. 25)

Hayford and Sealts show that chapter 25 (the hanging of Billy Budd) in its present form dates from a late stage, and indeed cannot have existed in its present length at any early stage (265-66). They show that the chapter originally ended with "the interchange between the purser and the surgeon" which later grew into a new chapter (265). The writing at the outset is conspicuously "fine," artful, literary. For many years Melville had been accustomed to sit pondering his engravings, some framed, probably many more loose in his portfolios. The canto "Prelusive" in *Clarel* (2.35) describes the Italian artist Piranesi's "rarer prints," the prison sequence, in language very like that of the first sentence of chapter 25. In *Clarel* "long tier on tier" of shadowed galleries impend over "cloisters, cloisters without end." Here in chapter 25 of *Billy Budd* the second sentence introduces a biblical comparison in a highly conventional image of night transferring its robe to the day—biblical imagery (from II Kings 2), not the expected pagan imagery. The light that appears in the east is meek and shy, but nothing supernatural happens. The sound is not of God's angel commanding Abraham to stay his arm, for instance, but bells being struck to declare it to be four in the morning, then there is the sound of silver whistles "summoning all hands to witness punishment" (122). Each man in the throng takes his place silently, and not in any particular arrangement, and without jostling, filling the deck between mainmast and foremast, the "powder-boys and younger tars" occupying the "summit" observatory of the "capacious launch" and black booms on either side of it while one watch of topmen has the great spectator spot of the rail of that "sea balcony" (122).

Billy's last words are a variation of what many a felon said before being hanged, the offering of a blessing on the captain having become a grimly ironic convention, made (sardonically or otherwise) by men invulnerable to any punishment beyond the one being carried out. Billy, we know, is incapable of irony, and the man who bade farewell to the *Rights-of-Man* now asks God to bless Captain Vere. The men, by a kind of reflex, echo Billy's words while Vere stands at rigid attention. The language used at the moment of the hanging is biblical, in a way which both ennobles the scene and draws back from any such ennoblement:

> At the same moment [as the silent signal for the hanging] it chanced that the vapory fleece hanging low in the East was shot through with a soft glory as of the fleece of the Lamb of God seen in mystical vision, and simultaneously therewith, watched by the wedged mass of upturned faces, Billy ascended; and, ascending, took the full rose of the dawn. (124)

But the fleece of clouds was only shot through with a soft glory that was "as" of the fleece of the Lamb of God seen in mystical vision (by the disciple John on the island of Patmos, in Revelation 1:14) and Billy did not ascend very far: as far as the yard-end. The only thing specified as abnormal about the scene is that Billy's body does not kick spasmodically, as usually happens, but is motionless. (Melville knew something about hangings from reading, and along with thousands of others—Charles Dickens was one— he witnessed the hanging of a notorious criminal couple in London in 1849; he may have known that hanging sometimes caused men's penises to become erect and ejaculate semen, and may have wanted to let any knowledgeable reader know that no such indignity occurred at Billy's death.)

## THE PURSER AND THE SURGEON (CH. 26)

Chapter 26, a late outgrowth of the previous chapter, is entirely devoted to the exchange ("some days afterwards") between the purser and the surgeon over the strange motionlessness of Billy's body (124). As Hayford and Sealts say (266), the subject was "long a pregnant one for Melville," the limitations of scientific men who make dubious claims to knowledge. They speculate cogently on the reason Melville might have let this afterthought stay in the text while deleting part of an elaboration about the chaplain and while wavering over whether or not to retain his "digression" on Nelson. Melville chose to write this scene as conversation, being in the habit, since much of his effort during the later stages of the work had been devoted to dramatizing scenes which he had first written as reflective. By the time he wrote this chapter he had long ago gotten rid of the "Lawyers, Experts, Clergy" section, and this chapter is part of the process by which those lines (important to him) were gradually used up elsewhere in the manuscript. For anyone wanting to interpret more than this isolated chapter (which seems designed to undercut the authority of the surgeon as a judge of Vere's behavior), it is important to realize that chapter 26 was written before chapter 20: the surgeon was developed here in chapter 26 as an object of satire for his pretensions to knowledge, and, when pushed into an intellectual corner by the persistent purser, makes his evasive escape in a manner reminiscent of Melville's arch-villain in *The Confidence-Man*. What the purser brings out, and what stands unrefuted by the surgeon, is that "the absence of spasmodic movement was phenomenal" (125). *Later* (260), Melville introduced a quite different characterization of the surgeon in chapter 20 and never reconciled that characterization with the one he had already drawn here in chapter 26. The effect of chapter 26 on the innocent reader is of course to some extent adventitious, not designed by Melville at all but merely accidental, occurring because he left the manuscript not quite complete. Readers who proceed from first page to last very reasonably expect any characterization of the surgeon in chapter 26 to build logically upon the way he was presented in chapter 20. That expectation is dashed.

### AFTER THE HANGING (CH. 27)

Chapter 27 was written before 26. Hayford and Sealts suppose it to have been first drafted at stage $X$ (266) (probably early in 1889?). What Melville describes is a sequence of three involuntary occurrences that momentarily threaten military order—one sound, another sound, one movement. The "silence" referred to in the first sentence (125) is that at the end of chapter 25, when the preconcerted signal for Billy's hanging was a "dumb one" and when no sailor uttered a sound (124). Following that silence was a sound which Melville frankly admits is "not easily to be verbally rendered" (126). Such an admission creates a sympathetic bond between the reader and the writer who is trying to convey something so difficult to put into words. Melville suggests that he may by analogy convey the sound to some people with a remarkable range of experience—anyone who in tropical mountains has heard the sound of "the freshet-wave of a torrent" during certain precise circumstances may be able to form "some conception of the sound now heard" (126). The strategy for conveying information may risk alienating the reader, for the number of readers who fall into the category specified are few indeed—fewer even than the limited number of readers who have made their adventurous way to such tropical mountains. Yet the narrator is clearly not desiring or welcoming such alienation; instead, he is intent on his task of analyzing:

> Being inarticulate, it was dubious in significance further than it seemed to indicate some capricious revulsion of thought or feeling such as mobs ashore are liable to, in the present instance possibly implying a sullen revocation on the men's part of their involuntary echoing of Billy's benediction. (126)

Discipline is instantly restored by the silver whistles of the boatswain and his mates.

Following the rapid, systematic burial of Billy's body at sea, a "second strange human murmur" is heard, now blended with "another inarticulate sound proceeding from certain larger seafowl" (127). Now, the second murmur unchecked, the superstitious sailors (of the age preceding ours, the narrator specifies, once again keeping hold of the significance of time and place), who had "just beheld the prodigy of repose in the form suspended in air," before it was deposited in the deep, make an "uncertain movement," a kind of "encroachment," although what is encroached upon is not specified (127). Suddenly the drum, this time, not the whistle, dissolves the mass of men. As Melville says, martial training makes obedience all but instinctive. Vere, the stickler for regulation, working with sailors who have been described also as sticklers for usage, has the men sent to quarters earlier than usual. In accounting for this "variance from usage" (127), Melville for the first time since the court martial enters Vere's mind (telling us that he deemed unusual action to be necessary) and quotes one of his habitual sayings:

> "With mankind," he would say, "forms, measured forms, are everything; and that is the import couched in the story of Or-

pheus with his lyre spellbinding the wild denizens of the wood."
And this he once applied to the disruption of forms going on
across the Channel and the consequences thereof. (128)

"This" apparently refers to Vere's belief that "measured forms"
are everything, and in application to events in France during and
following the Revolution the lesson is Burkean—chaos follows upon
the violation of established order. In the context of the manuscript
as it stood when Melville wrote these words, the view attributed to
Vere is hardly distinguishable from the one taken by the narrator.
(I avoid the misleading phrase "the manuscript as a whole," since
the phrase begs the question of whether or not the pages then
resting in separate folders were or were not part of the manuscript
as a whole.)

But Melville does not leave the scene without his realistic reminder that in keeping order here "music and religious rites"
subserved "the discipline and purposes of war" (128). Furthermore, any apparent mysticism about the fleece-like appearance of
clouds is banished, for at full day the fleece "of low-hanging"
(probably only an unintended verbal reminder of Billy's fate) "va-
por had vanished, licked up by the sun that late had so glorified
it" (128). Maybe a special meaning of "to glorify" is involved here,
to give a kind of halo; in any case, the glory is gone, and in a
strange concluding sentence Melville describes the "circumambi-
ent air in the clearness of its serenity" as "like smooth white
marble in the polished block not yet removed from the marble-
dealer's yard" (128)—a comparison that can only remind the
reader that Billy's grave is in the unstable water.

## THE DEATH OF CAPTAIN VERE (CH. 28)

Chapter 28, not just inscribed but first composed during stage
*X* (267), recounts the fight between the *Bellipotent* and the French
ship, the *Atheist*, in which Vere is wounded. Taken ashore at Gi-
braltar, he dies, drugged with morphine or opium, murmuring
"Billy Budd, Billy Budd" (129). Melville stresses that "these were
not the accents of remorse" (129).

Chapter 28 recurs at the outset to the much earlier denial that
this story is a romance. The "symmetry of form attainable in pure
fiction" is not something the reader should expect in "a narration

essentially having less to do with fable than with fact" (128). What Melville meant to achieve by this warning is by no means clear. The effect of the reference to literary form is perhaps unintentionally tinged with the powerful saying just attributed to Vere ("forms, measured forms, are everything" with mankind). In literature, is measured form everything? Plainly not, for Melville announces (128) an aesthetics of imperfection ("ragged edges") and even incompleteness (not always finished off with an "architectural finial"). In this fiction Melville claims a literal truth-telling: "How it fared with the Handsome Sailor during the year of the Great Mutiny has been faithfully given" (128). As writer, Melville now talks in terms of three "brief chapters" "in way of sequel" (128). Does it matter to the reader that in fact this has not been and is not to be a true story? Do Melville's claims for truth distract from the believability of his story? Readers will weigh the effects for themselves before answering such questions.

## THE NEWS ACCOUNT (CH. 29)

Chapter 29, Hayford and Sealts show, belongs to a very early stage of composition, long before Vere had any developed part in the story (268). During the middle phases of Melville's work on the book, this chapter, the news account, stood last and the ballad preceded it (268). For some of that time the chapter (and the whole of the story as it stood) ended with an addition (268), what Hayford and Sealts call the "coda" ("Here ends a story not unwarranted by what sometimes happens in this incongruous [?] world of ours—Innocence and infamy, spiritual depravity and fair repute." [Plate VIII (opposite p. 5) and 422]). Melville did not recast the news account to fit his later developments of the narrative, a fact which, as Hayford and Sealts show, created anomalies in the text:

> The news account, since it was written . . . before Captain Vere's role was developed . . . makes no mention of his part in the affair of "the tenth of the last month," or of the engagement with the French ship (which would have been very soon after), or of his mortal wound, or his death—although all of these would have had to be known to anyone in a position to originate the report from which the account stemmed. As a matter of fact, since

everybody aboard, as the later development had it, knew at least the "outside" story of the case and sympathized with Billy, no imaginable informant could have given "in good faith" a report subject to such diametric distortion as that displayed in the news account. These matters that were developed later than the composition of the account make its last sentence, particularly, anachronistic: "Nothing amiss is now apprehended aboard. . . ." That Melville was aware of something of the sort seems implied in his pencil notation at the head of the first leaf (Leaf 340), "Speak of the fight & death of Captain Vere". He never went on to do so by revising the account, but canceled the notation. (It must be said that no critic has noted the omission.) (269)

Thus the impulse which made Melville bring the prose headnote to the ballad in line with the events he had finally described in the story also emerged as he reflected, at least for a passing moment, on what would be needed to salvage chapter 29 as the middle one of three concluding chapters rather than the final chapter of the book. But if he fully realized that he needed to resolve the inconsistency, he had not actually resolved it before he died. (Vaguely or specifically realizing that something needs to be done does not count; what counts is actually making the change or addition and working it into the "manuscript as a whole.")

Despite the expansions of the story that left it illogical, chapter 29, even as Melville left it, retains some of its original function. The inconsistencies, obvious as they are once Hayford and Sealts have pointed them out, do not destroy the news account's primary function of showing how the world will inevitably misconstrue complex human events. It hardly matters to the reader (it plainly does *not* matter to the reader, since no critic—no *professional reader*—noticed a problem), when he or she is caught up in the story, that the chapter impossibly purports to be based on information from an insider. Before Hayford and Sealts published their analysis, readers unthinkingly accepted the substance of the chapter as something outsiders would well say and believe. Readers of the Hayford-Sealts edition, with its full title of *Billy Budd, Sailor (An Inside Narrative)*, apparently continue to take the chapter the same way, whether or not they have read the editors' analysis of the anomalies.

At least readers have not been in the intolerable position of trying to make sense of something that does not fit the story at all;

they are able to screen out the meaningless details of the chapter and seize on the essence. To be sure, they are accepting the impossible, but they are not perverting the intention Melville had in writing the news account to stand as the final chapter or the different, imperfect intention he had in placing it as the middle of three after-the-fact chapters. Imperfect as chapter 29 is, it achieves some of its basic function in the new placement: while chapter 28 focuses on the inner thoughts of a single character, Vere, the news account broadens the focus to include most of those contemporaries who will learn of Billy Budd; and the last chapter narrows again to the ephemeral ballad which, though factually untrue of Billy's life and death, remains, at least for a time, as the way he is remembered among his fellows. Only the whole book, the "inside narrative" told by Melville (but does that include the Nelson chapter?), offers any hope of setting the true story on permanent human record, and the book itself respects the final mystery of all human motives and actions. The fact remains that chapter 29 does not make full sense in the context where it stands.

## MEMORIES OF BILLY, AND THE BALLAD (CH. 30)

When Melville placed the ballad to follow the news account, Hayford and Sealts show, he could no longer use whatever had introduced it, so he drafted a new prose paragraph. One of the themes is the recurrent one of misconstruing and reading aright. Here the sailors who treat a chip of the spar from which Billy was hung as if it were a chip of the Cross do so in ignorance of "the secret facts of the tragedy" but in intuitive confidence that Billy was "as incapable of mutiny as of wilful murder" (131). While the news account in chapter 29 now mainly consists of a wholly mistaken report said to have been written in good faith, chapter 30 deals at the start with traditions which survived at least for "some few years" (131) among Billy's shipmates, and these traditions have a basis in truth. Billy in the last chapter is, after all, understood—up to a point. Melville ascribes the ballad to a man of Billy's own watch, and the ballad, drafted long before Billy's characterization was developed, does not go far toward capturing what was memorable about Billy Budd. Only Melville's account does that, and it now stands (in the words that end chapter 29), "in human record to attest what manner of men respectively were John Claggart and Billy Budd" (131). (Vere, not developed at the time these words were drafted, was never worked into them.)

P · A · R · T        F · O · U · R

---

# Textual Problems and Interpretation

---

ONCE THE "WORK" KNOWN AS *BILLY BUDD* ENTERED LITERARY DISCUS-
sion there was no way of compartmentalizing what was said and
thought about the slightly varying texts that Weaver prepared in
1924 and again in 1928, or the slightly varying text that F. Barron
Freeman prepared in 1948 or the texts prepared under the guidance of corrigenda to Freeman in the 1950s, or the Hayford-Sealts
text of 1962, or even to the variant text which Milton Stern "edited" from the Hayford-Sealts Genetic Text in 1975. To refer to
*Billy Budd* is to refer quite specifically to a quite amorphous group
of entities: texts entitled *Billy Budd, Foretopman* are not necessarily identical with each other, texts entitled *Billy Budd, Sailor* are
not necessarily identical (partly because typographical errors frequently occur in authorized reprintings, partly because the University of Chicago Press permitted Stern to use the final title as established by Hayford and Sealts), and of course any text so far entitled
*Billy Budd, Foretopman* differs in fairly obvious ways from any text
so far entitled *Billy Budd, Sailor.* In this historical miasma it becomes exceedingly difficult to distinguish the factitiously problematical from the inherently problematical in discussing the history
of the reputation, interpretation, and significance of *Billy Budd*
(whatever that is).

Therefore after my reading of *Billy Budd, Sailor* I want to
confront again the textual problems (and resulting interpretive
problems) created by Weaver's faulty transcription of the manuscript, then to confront the inherently problematical nature of the
text as Melville left it. How much time should we spend talking

about a page and a quarter that Melville discarded from his manuscript and that Weaver mistakenly printed not only as still a part of the story but as perhaps its single most conspicuous feature, its "Preface"? How much time should we spend talking about another, smaller discarded section (on "Lawyers, Experts, Clergy") that took up a third of a page when Weaver mistakenly included it in the Constable Edition? How much time should we spend talking about the entire chapter 4, on Nelson, which Melville removed from the manuscript at an early stage and never quite brought himself to restore to the manuscript, though Weaver, Freeman, and Hayford-Sealts all print it as part of the text? How much time should we spend emphasizing that the story as we have it (in whatever form we have it) is incomplete?

## TEXTUAL PROBLEMS CREATED BY WEAVER

There is no ideal place in this book for talking about the issues created by the presence of a spurious "preface" in *Billy Budd, Foretopman*. After the Chicago edition was published there would be no use talking about the "preface" if the words printed in 1924 as a preface had not entered at once into the history of criticism on the book, if later New Critical readings had not often used the so-called preface in arguing that it had (as one might reasonably expect) prefatory functions, and if post–Hayford and Sealts critics had not sometimes demonstrated a most curious attachment to the "preface"—behaving as if without it they could not proceed to look further at the words of the story. I did not discuss it at the start of my chapter-by-chapter reading of *Billy Budd, Sailor* because it is not in that text, either as preface or as part of chapter 19, where it once stood. In discussing it here I want to avoid creating the impression that it is crucially important in the interpretation of *Billy Budd, Sailor*. I have chosen to discuss the problems involving the "preface" here, although it requires me to treat together different groups of readers from 1924 to the present.

There are always very curious effects from any gross blunder in publishing (such as the disastrous accident whereby the "Epilogue" was lost from *The Whale*, the English edition of *Moby-Dick*, thereby exposing Melville to ridicule from hostile reviewers and exasperation from reviewers who wanted to like the book but could not stomach the use of a first-person narrator in a story where the narrator seems not to survive the catastrophe). Editorial blunders can be fascinating also, and not just for the petty imp in us who delights to see stuffy people exposed as foolish. An editorial blunder like Weaver's, where a rejected passage from a late chapter was placarded as a preface, can tell us an enormous amount about us all as readers.

Many modern theorists talk about "valorizing" and "privileging" parts of a story, terms that aptly apply to what all readers do with prefaces. Prefaces obviously point forward, but their function does not end when the reader proceeds to the first and second chapters. They continue to guide readers long after the readers have read beyond the preface into the rest of the story. Part of the reading process, even when the reader is impelled to turn each page in eagerness to reach the end, involves "reference." The literal Latin sense is *carrying back*, and at times a reader feels the need to go back, to make reference to, the preface, if only to reassure himself that he knows where he is headed, or more often a reader may merely make mental re-flection to the opening, *valorized* words of a preface. The Weaver "Preface" set up false expectations, set up an adventitious reading experience, insofar as the book was read (and then taught) in the light of the preface.

The strains the Weaver and Freeman texts put on the unsuspecting reader become clear when we look at the "preface" for its prefatory functions. (For a reading text of the full passage see p. 135 above.) At first it seems to function adequately. It begins "The year 1797, the year of this narrative" (377), and the title page of the Weaver text has already announced that the story is to be about what befell one "Billy Budd, Foretopman," in "the year of the great mutiny," so Weaver's readers saw the opening of the "preface" as a confirmation of the information in the subtitle. That relationship between the subtitle Weaver used (an intermediate subtitle) and a rejected portion of chapter 19 was of course accidental, adventitious, not planned by Melville, but it "worked," and in something close to an authorial fashion: Melville, after all, had wanted the subtitle (when that *was* still the subtitle) to precede a similar opening: "In the time before steamships" (43). So the discarded fragment seems at first to "work" perfectly well when given a prefatory position. It contains straightforward historical dating and reflections, and seems to be tied to the subtitle.

Still, a careful reader might have wondered about what the "preface" was prefacing—for it declares 1797 the year of the narrative, then seems to look forward to treating in some way the ambiguous humanitarian advances that may have followed the entire Revolutionary era, from 1789 through 1815. Nothing of the sort happens in the rest of the Weaver text. But in another way the words (which, to repeat, Melville never at any moment intended to be a preface and which he rejected from *any* place in the manuscript) were distinctly unprefatorial. They are, after all, oddly irresolute. In an effort to dispense even-handed judgment the narrator recalls the "hereditary wrongs" which drove the French to revolt (377). Then he recalls that the Revolution itself became a worse wrongdoer and led to the excesses of the Napoleonic empire. Then he concludes the first paragraph with a sentence that at first seems to be going to say that the ultimate outcome was "a political advance along nearly the whole line for Europeans" (378). I say "at first" because of the construction "During those years not the wisest could have foreseen" (378); when you start a sentence that way you imply that something unforeseen by even the wise has really come to pass, but that initial expectation is not fulfilled, for what Melville goes on to say is that what the wisest could not have foreseen has in fact only "apparently" turned out to be an advance, or specifically "a political advance"; he substitutes "To some thinkers" for "apparently" (making the advance only the opinion of "some thinkers" not all later thinkers, the wisest or not); and he qualifies even the sort of political advance that the outcome "apparently" or "to some thinkers" turned out to be: it was not an advance for all mankind, or even an advance along the whole line for Europeans, but an advance "along nearly the whole line for Europeans" (378). The foregoing analysis does not fully describe the sequence of Melville's initial inscriptions and subsequent alterations in this contorted passage which he himself (as Hayford and Sealts say [378]) left "incoherent."

Melville for many years had been the master of playing with the difference between what seemed and what was, as well as the difference between what seemed to some and what seemed to all. This passage from the opening of "The Town-Ho's Story" (ch. 54

of *Moby-Dick*) is a perfect example of Melville's ability to combine suggestiveness with evasiveness:

> To some the general interest in the White Whale was now wildly heightened by a circumstance of the Town-Ho's story, which seemed obscurely to involve with the whale a certain wondrous, inverted visitation of one of those so called judgments of God which at times are said to overtake some men. (242)

A reader of the Weaver text of *Billy Budd, Foretopman* could reasonably conclude that Melville in the first paragraph of what was printed as the "preface" was setting up a similarly dubious situation which was to govern the entire story. That assumption would of course be fallacious, for Melville's intentions in that paragraph were more *local*: his intentions as he drafted the paragraph were focused on how the words would function in the place he was inscribing them (in a passage now numbered ch. 19), and as he inscribed the paragraph or the next or *after* he inscribed them, he was so dissatisfied with how they seemed to function there that he removed them (although they plainly contained ideas which had not ceased to interest him).

The second paragraph of the "preface" in Weaver's edition offers a seemingly coherent parallel to the first paragraph. The French spirit of revolt inflamed sailors on British ships to "rise against real abuses" at Spithead and later to make "inordinate and aggressive demands" at the Nore, and yet in a way good came out of evil again: "doubtless" the Great Mutiny "gave the first latent prompting to most important reforms in the British navy" (378). Since this paragraph begins "Now as elsewhere hinted" (378), the reader can naturally take these words as a promise of something to come, but the story that follows is *not* in any important way about naval abuses which led to mutiny (even Billy's impressment is not presented as abuse, in strong contrast to the way Melville had long ago presented his title character in *Israel Potter* [1855] as a victim of impressment). When Melville wrote the words, when the passage was still a part of his working manuscript, he of course was recalling the reader's attention to something he had written *earlier* and which *still was placed earlier* in the story. Although the words initially make sufficient sense in the Weaver text as a promise of something to come, the promise is not kept. What if a reader of the Weaver text were by nature the sort of person who pays attention to all promises in real life and in real literature, and looked forward to a narrative that would deal with political advances which grew out of the Revolutionary period? That person blessed or cursed with a retentive memory and faith in the sanctity of promises would have grounds for extreme dissatisfaction as he or she progressed toward the end of the text, for the apparent promise is never fulfilled. Like the first paragraph, the second is inconclusive when misused as the preface for the story of Billy Budd.

So if one takes the so-called preface seriously for its prefatory functions, one finds in it a somewhat fuzzy narratorial stance. Insofar as the two paragraphs have, in their placement in some editions, a prefatory function, that is an obscuring function. Except for the fact that the first sentence specifies that the year of the narrative is 1797, one could suspect from the content of the two paragraphs that a major focus of the following narrative would be ultimate general reforms paradoxically initiated by revolution in France and mutiny on British ships and coming to fruition much later, far into the nineteenth century. The section seems to set up the reader to expect a story about a real mutiny grounded in serious naval abuses, a mutiny put down by execution (something, the Weaver subtitle said, "befell" Billy Budd, and the "preface" talks of hanging the ringleaders of the mutiny as "an admonitory spectacle"). The reader seems to be warned that only by taking a long historical view can even "some" thinkers decide that a monstrous mutiny could ("doubtless") eventuate in "reforms." Now, there is nothing inherently uninteresting in this outline. Indeed, one can see great narrative possibilities in it. But the fact is that Melville himself did not see such possibilities in the two paragraphs. The very inconclusiveness, the evenhandedness, is what made the section inappropriate at the spot where Melville drafted the words to fit. Because he had been led into irresolution which distracted from his progress in the story, he removed the passage. Weaver therefore offered (in all innocence) a text which has since turned out to be a test of what we as readers (also innocent) do when confronted with something which doesn't belong where we see it and was never meant to belong there: we make the best of an imperfect situation and we never say (not a single critic of Billy Budd, Foretopman ever said), "This preface does not function as a preface."

The second passage of any length which Melville had discarded and which Weaver mistakenly put back into the text is the one Melville had entitled "Lawyers, Experts, Clergy" when it stood at the start of what Hayford and Sealts number as chapter 12. In going through Melville's papers his widow found two superseded leaves (H-S numbers 353-54) which she recognized as from *Billy Budd*. She made a memo to "Find proper place for insertion" (338). Weaver accepted her judgment that the pages were to be reinserted rather than analyzing the growth of the manuscript in a way that would have revealed that they were in fact superseded. He printed them in his chapter 10 (ch. 11 in the Chicago numbering) as the third paragraph from the end, between the paragraph beginning "Now something" and the one beginning "Dark sayings":

> Can it be this phenomenon, disowned or not acknowledged, that in some criminal cases puzzles the courts? For this cause have our juries at times not only to endure the prolonged contentions of lawyers with their fees, but also the yet more perplexing strife of the medical experts with theirs? But why leave it to them? Why not subpoena as well the clerical proficients? Their vocation bringing them into peculiar contact with so many human beings, and sometimes in their least guarded hour, in interviews very much more confidential than those of physician and patient; this would seem to qualify them to know something about those intricacies involved in the question of moral responsibility; whether in a given case, say, the crime proceeded from mania in the brain or rabies of the heart. As to any differences among themselves these clerical proficients might develop on the stand, these could hardly be greater than the direct contradictions exchanged between the remunerated medical experts. (46-47)

When it stood in the manuscript, not later than the *E* stage, this passage was really two paragraphs below where Weaver put it, after the "Dark sayings" paragraph and after the next one, "The point of the story turning," and part of the time while it was in the manuscript, at least, it stood as a separate chapter entitled "Lawyers, Experts, Clergy." Weaver was not only wrong to have reinserted it at all, he compounded his error slightly by putting it in a little earlier than it ever went.

The "Lawyers, Experts, Clergy" section has a complicated effect on any reader who encounters it in the Weaver or Freeman text of chapter 10 (the reader of course will not encounter it in the Hayford and Sealts text, where it would have appeared in the chapter they number 12, if Melville had not discarded it). The passage seems valuable as conveying information—information on a topic fresh today, when the legal status of "expert witnesses" is being challenged anew, with evidence being produced that psychologists and psychiatrists who offer expert testimony in courtrooms have only an average chance of predicting, for instance, whether a rapist will be more or less likely than other rapists to rape again when free. There is great appeal in Melville's opinion of these experts—any skeptical look at the value of what we can expect from the testimony of expert witnesses satisfies one side of our always divided attitude toward experts: we tend to accept their pronouncements without question, but we also live with at least a rankling, suppressed sense that they are putting something over on the rest of us. When we read passages which appeal to our own latent suspicions of experts, we offer our alert attention, and remember the passages as we read on. Long before, in *The Confidence-Man* (1857), Melville had held up to scorn those practitioners of pseudosciences who claimed to read human nature with facility. He was familiar with Ralph Waldo Emerson's outrage, memorably expressed in the "Temperament" section of the essay "Experience," against those who claim scientific competence to predict human behavior from such "evidence" as the bumps on the skull (then being learnedly "read" by the faddish phrenologists):

> Temperament puts all divinity to rout. I know the mental proclivity of physicians. I hear the chuckle of the phrenologists. Theoretic kidnappers and slavedrivers, they esteem each man the victim of another, who winds him round his finger by knowing the law of his being, and by such cheap signboards as the color of his beard, or the slope of his occiput, reads the inventory of his fortunes and character. The grossest ignorance does not disgust like this impudent knowingness.

Like Emerson, Melville saw learned experts as trivializing and dehumanizing human nature by reducing people to some psychological or physiological formula. In this case, Melville very likely removed the little passage because having it in the manuscript upset him. There is a family tradition, and some evidence, that a physical examination which Melville underwent in the mid-1850s at the hands of his friend Dr. Oliver Wendell Holmes was understood by some in the family to be an attempt to determine whether or not Melville were insane. If such an examination occurred, or if a physical examination were interpreted as being an examination for insanity, then it is understandable both that Melville wrote the intense little section and later removed it. Beyond question the topic rankled in him, for much later as he wrote the passage on the closeness of sanity to insanity in chapter 21 he commented on the willingness of "some professional experts" to pronounce their judgments on such delicate matters: "There is nothing namable but that some men will, or undertake to, do it for pay" (102).

When Melville removed "Lawyers, Experts, Clergy," he saved it and later he managed to work some of the ideas into the story in less self-exposing contexts. (See the discussion of ch. 16, above.) The "men of the world" (87) at the end of that chapter may be the sophisticates Melville had already identified as "lawyers, experts, clergy"—a possibility that points up one of the vicissitudes of hit-or-miss revision. An author can eliminate a passage and then can even obviate it in the most thorough fashion by "using it up," incorporating the essence of it into another passage so that if restored to the text the omitted passage would create redundancies— all this can happen, and yet while the passage stood in the work the author could have built in allusions to it, allusions which may or may not have been altered after the later decision to use up the passage and to delete it from the manuscript. For an author or an editor, getting rid of a significant passage without leaving loose ends is harder than one would think, simply because unity really is built in, little by little, during the act of composition. The Genetic Text offers little evidence because this particular passage belongs to a fairly late stage of inscription (and also of composition) and was little revised after inscription.

My parallel between the "Lawyers, Experts, Clergy" passage and chapter 16 is tentatively drawn. The evidence is much stronger for Melville's reuse of some of the rejected material in chapter 21. As Hayford and Sealts show (263), Melville "recurred to the topic of professional 'experts' testifying"; "in effect, he salvaged and reused the topic of 'experts' from that episode as he had already used its other materials (the jury puzzled by the question of motivation) at $X$ in constituting the trial scene which ensues." This process is familiar to anyone who writes a term paper: we may sacrifice a strong paragraph because we cannot fit it into a larger context, but we may manage to cannibalize part of the paragraph in what we put in its place or in what we put elsewhere in the paper. The fact that Melville "salvaged and reused the topic" made for strange, inadvertent effects when Weaver restored the superseded "Lawyers, Experts, Clergy" but also included the passages Melville later cannibalized from it.

The upshot is that if we are using *Billy Budd* in a highly specialized college course on, say, the relationship between textual evidence and literary interpretation, or an even more ambitiously esoteric course on textual evidence, criticism, and literary theory, then we could readily justify spending classroom time on what Weaver printed as the "preface" and the lines he printed on lawyers, experts, and clergy. Such a class could explore how critics have been able to write about the non-preface as if it were designed as a preface and what they have seen as its prefatory functions. Such a class could determine if the Genetic Text can reveal the full process by which Melville removed the lines on lawyers, experts, and clergy then *used them up*, working their essence into later portions (if he really did that). Such a class could look at the even more challenging relationship between either the "1797" leaves or the "experts" lines and the rest of the text, and try to determine from the Genetic Text whether or not Melville, while those passages still stood in the text, had worked into later-written portions (no matter where they stand) some references to them which he never revised out of the text after removing these two sections. There is a considerable amount to be learned about the creative process and an unlimited amount to be learned about the reading process from such evidence, particularly if a teacher were to explore similar situations involving some other textually problematical novels which have evoked a body of problematical criticism. Some of us become immoderately excited about such textual-critical-theoretical questions, and I confess now, as I finish this book, that I wish I had included an analysis of *Billy Budd, Sailor* in my *Flawed Texts and Verbal Icons: Literary Authority in American Fiction* (1984). The likelihood that few people will ever teach such a course in the aesthetic implications of textual evidence does not mean that it cannot be exciting and enlightening.

But the textual problems involving *Billy Budd* which might prove fascinating to students of the history and practice of literary criticism and theory (or, to name other specialized audiences, students of the psychology and physiology of reading) do not *necessarily* have anything at all to do with either Melville's intentions or with the meaning of *Billy Budd*. If we are interested in "reading" *Billy Budd* for two days in a survey course, there is no good reason to focus for long on the unambiguously discarded sections—especially not if that means we will neglect the parts of the story which Melville not only wrote but indubitably left in the manuscript. It is dismayingly and humiliatingly easy to fall into the trap of letting previous critics define our terms of discussion, so that we talk about one or two trivial textual cruxes at such length that a stranger to the discussion would think they were the heart of the manuscript. And the disproportion has ill-effects in two directions: in talking about two little hunks of prose Melville discarded we tend to ignore all the other sentences, phrases, and single words which Melville wrote but later revised out of the manuscript (a word or a phrase at a time), and we tend to talk less (and think less) about all the words which he did *not* discard but kept in the text.

## THE INHERENTLY PROBLEMATICAL NATURE OF THE TEXT

Unfortunately for any lover of perfect literary works, not all the textual problems of *Billy Budd* are factitious, the result of editorial error. Other problems are inherent in the manuscript as Melville left it. As we have seen, Hayford and Sealts explain (246) that Melville interpolated the Nelson chapter, rejected it, vacillated several times, and even revised it while he had it separated from the manuscript, in a folder, but never restored it to the manuscript. We cannot separate the problem that the Nelson chapter was removed (and never unequivocally put back in) from the problem that at his death Melville left the story uncompleted in still other ways, with the characterization of Vere going in quite different directions. And the Nelson chapter affects how we read *all* the passages on Vere which Melville left in the text; it really is crucial to any full discussion of the meaning of the story. Even if we resent having the critics of a previous generation or two define for us the terms in which we have to talk about *Billy Budd*, we are to some extent trapped: we have to face these problems before we get on with our own attempts to grapple with the text.

The Hayford-Sealts decision to include chapter 4 is defensible and indeed wholly justifiable according to editorial theory and practice, but the aesthetic consequences of having it in the text need to be confronted again. Without the Nelson chapter, and without the late pencil revisions, the story is fully interpretable. *With* the Nelson chapter and without the late pencil revisions the story is adequately interpretable, with Vere being much like Nelson but not quite of his heroic order. However, after Melville made the late pencil revisions that undercut Vere's character, the story became extremely difficult if not impossible to interpret as a whole, since clues as to how to read Vere's behavior were left going in two (or more than two?) directions. With the late pencil revisions in the text and with the Nelson chapter put back into the text from the separate folder where Melville had kept it during the last stages of his work on the story, then not only is Vere's behavior questioned, even worse, the contrast with Nelson's behavior seems (to any attentive reader) to have been set up to make us, from early in the story, see Vere as much inferior to Nelson, who could brilliantly, bravely, and patriotically (we tell ourselves) have done what Vere never thought of doing: could have pardoned Billy on the spot and then publicly told the crew why, and have won them to his command in doing so.

Once Harrison Hayford and Merton M. Sealts, Jr., had provided a reliable text of *Billy Budd, Sailor*, this story ceased to be one which had to be read, if read at all, in a faulty text. The only caveat is that the text, as the editors stressed, still had to be read in a text which the author had not quite finished. They laid out the small and large ways in which it was unfinished. Among other minor inconsistencies that Melville left unresolved they listed (256) the problem of whether or not the afterguardsman and Billy recognize each other in encounters subsequent to the temptation scene. At one point a change in metaphor (258) introduced "an unnoticed inconsistency with the allusion to 'pitfal[l] under the clover.'" In chapter 21 Melville's revisions created an inconsistency concerning "the number and personnel of the court" (262), and a much more serious one concerning whether or not Vere's behavior was according to usage. Melville noticed the first of these and tried to remedy the situation, but became so tangled up that "inadvertently he left in his final version the inconsistency as to both the number and personnel of the court" (262). He did not try to resolve the more serious inconsistency.

We have already looked at Hayford and Sealts's lucid description of the most conspicuous *localized* inconsistency left in the story, the imperfectly functioning news account in chapter 29. Their brilliant analysis needs to be pondered, particularly that deadpan line which closes it, the comment that no critic had mentioned any problem with the chapter. The most important regard in which *Billy Budd* is not complete, the Chicago editors made clear, is that in his last revisions Melville altered his previously consistent characterization of Vere. In their "Perspectives for Criticism" the editors make the reasonable observation that "were it not for the effect of Melville's late pencil revisions" involving the character of Vere, then "the critical controversy of the last dozen years [since about 1950] over the story's tone in relation to Vere and his actions would scarcely have arisen" (34). If he had intended to keep that last characterization and work it back through the earlier parts of the work in which he had depicted Vere, he did not live to do any of that revisionary harmonizing: the earlier scenes stood as he had left them before his "late pencil revisions." Hayford and Sealts elaborated this reasonable-sounding notion of how critics would have responded to a more coherent text:

> Even those interpreters who disapprove Vere's course could not well question the author's evident design as revealed at Stage *Ga*, to establish that course in terms of "existing conditions in the navy." The cumulative effect—whatever the intention—of his subsequent deletions and insertions, however, was to throw into doubt not only the rightness of Vere's decision and the soundness of his mind but also the narrator's own position concerning him. As the revised sequence now stands, it is no longer as narrator but in terms of the surgeon's reflections that Melville introduces the reaction to Vere and his plan to place Billy on trial. He leaves the narrator pointedly noncommittal, telling the reader in so many words that he must decide for himself concerning the captain's state of mind. Yet in the unmodified para-

graphs that Melville allowed to stand immediately after the surgeon's reflections, the narrator presents Vere's position in a
sympathetic tone (Leaves 238-45). Also, following the narrator's
allusion to the *Somers* case as "History, and here cited without
comment," Melville retained a quotation from "a writer whom
few know" (obviously Melville himself), the tenor of which is
exculpatory, or at worst extenuative. The next chapter (Ch. 22),
also retained after the revision, reports Vere's closeted interview
with Billy in a tone unmistakably favorable to the captain. In
sum, it is the late revisions—those involving the surgeon—which
raise doubts; those passages composed earlier which are still retained tend to represent Vere favorably. (34-35)

Hayford and Sealts in their section on "Perspectives for Criticism"
made it clear that some lines of criticism would be dead ends for
any critic taking them, but their tone was not negative or admonitory. They looked forward, with some eagerness, to criticism that
would not be a waste of time for the writers of essays and the
readers of essays but would build upon the factual basis they had
established. They were rather young, still, and were optimistic.
They had done a formidable amount of extremely difficult work,
some of it drudgery but some of it strenuously challenging them
to reevaluate their own training in order to expand their scholarly
and aesthetic notions to cover the reality of their discoveries. Prod-
ucts of an earlier Yale decade when Stanley T. Williams, the biog-
rapher of Washington Irving, was directing archival research for a
series of dissertations on Melville, they were out of touch with the
Yale of the 1950s and early 1960s, when it had become the bastion
of the New Criticism (before it became a bastion of phenomenology then deconstructionist theory). They simply had no notion of
how hard it would be for critics to deal with their evidence that
*Billy Budd* was not complete. They thought that such serious work
would be taken into account by all subsequent writers on *Billy
Budd*. That, as we have seen, did not happen.

All of us as readers tend to resist being told that what we have
read with full satisfaction does not in fact make sense, or does not
quite make good sense, or makes only a skewed sort of sense, yet
evidence such as that quoted from Hayford and Sealts in the previous paragraph is irrefutable. We are, as readers and just as human beings, hopelessly defensive, yet often enough when what we

are reading does not quite make sense we blame ourselves, not the work we are reading. Literature comes perfectly packaged, and perfect inside the package, we think. But very often literature is inescapably the flawed product of brave and heroic but finally imperfect human effort. Many examples make it clear that we refuse, in reading, to blame the text for any bewilderment we are feeling (usually, we know from experience, the fault is ours, and if we try harder we can understand what looks incomprehensible). Cognitive psychologists can help account for the way we read imperfect texts, for they show that the mind tends to impose meaning when vital clues to meaning are absent or else to impose meaning at the cost of denying the existence of ambiguity. (See especially chs. 12-14 in James J. Gibson's 1966 study *The Senses Considered as Perceptual Systems.*) Readers are not being morally reprehensible or (worse) short on basic intelligence but are simply being human when they ignore discrepancies and ambiguities in their advance toward arriving at an orderly sense of their experience of a text. So it was not the New Criticism which impelled readers to make sense of any text they held in their hands—it is the nature of the beast, the perceptual systems we are born with, which predispose us to make sense of what we see, even, experiments have shown, if we have to undergo the stress of screening out elements in a field of vision—whether a primeval landscape or a page open before us—which do not readily make sense. Even as we are trained to become "close readers," our primitive assumption that things should make sense and our sophisticated theoretical conviction that things make sense work together to make us boggle at trivial oddities such as variant spellings while ignoring greater discrepancies such as gaps or severe truncations. As readers we routinely strain out the textual gnats but swallow the camels.

Our task, having absorbed some of the lessons of Hayford and Sealts in their study of *Billy Budd, Sailor*, is to acknowledge the fact that when we read their text we are dealing with a work that is not quite finished, that contains a number of small contradictions, that contains clues as to the behavior of a main character, Captain Vere, which seem to lead both to favorable and to unfavorable judgments, and that contains at least one important chapter, the one on Lord Nelson, which the author might have left out of the book if he had lived to print it. The other part of our task is to acknowledge that there are limits to what we can responsibly say about such a text. We cannot and should not stop reading *Billy Budd, Sailor* as a classic work of American literature, but we should acknowledge that we do not help our reputation as readers and do not help the reputation of the work when we act as if we can offer a complete, coherent interpretation of it. There are some things we can't honestly say about *Billy Budd* (we cannot celebrate the consistency of characterization, for instance, or even the perfect unity of theme and structure). So much for limitations: the good news is that dazzling insights await any good reader of the Hayford-Sealts Reading Text and their Genetic Text. Melville said it best in book 4 ("Retrospective") of *Pierre*: "Something ever comes of all persistent inquiry; we are not so continually curious for nothing."

# A Melville Chronology

(BASED ON *THE NEW MELVILLE LOG*)

1819    Herman Melvill (as the name was spelled) is born in New York
        City on 1 August, third child of Allan Melvill (a Boston-reared
        merchant, son of a still-living "Indian" of the Tea Party,
        Thomas Melvill, immortalized by young Oliver Wendell
        Holmes in 1831 as "The Last Leaf") and Maria Gansevoort
        (daughter of the late General Peter Gansevoort of Albany, the
        hero of the defense of Fort Stanwix in the Revolution). The
        Melvill family was closely allied with noble Scottish families,
        and claimed royal blood. The Gansevoorts were complexly
        related to all the great Dutch families who had dominated
        upstate New York since the late seventeenth century.

1825    Attends New York Male High School.

1827    Makes a summer visit to his Melvill grandparents in Boston.

1828    Is named the best speaker in the introductory department at
        the Male High School.

1829    Makes a second summer visit to his grandparents in Boston;
        in September is enrolled in the Grammar School of Columbia
        College.

1830    After his father's failure in business and move to Albany, at-
        tends Albany Academy.

1832    After his father's death in January is withdrawn from school
        and put to work as a clerk at New York State Bank in Albany.
        His older brother Gansevoort starts a fur and cap business in

Albany. When cholera strikes Albany in the summer, his mother takes all eight children to safety at the Pittsfield, Massachusetts farm of his uncle Thomas Melvill, but at her brother Peter's insistence she sends Herman back into danger in order to safeguard his job. [From this time, Pittsfield was a "Paradise" to the widow and her children, a place of gorgeous landscape, pure air, abundant summer fruit, and enough cousins for every child to have a crony.]

1833   Herman gets to spend a week's vacation in Pittsfield.

1834   Winter, Herman continues at the bank; summer, he clerks in Gansevoort's fur and cap store, with no vacation.

1835   Herman clerks in Gansevoort's store and follows his brother into the Albany Young Men's Association; summer, cousins Thomas W. Melvill and Leonard Gansevoort, both resigned from the navy, join the crews of whaling ships; fall, Herman enters the Albany Classical School [?].

1836   August, Herman spends his vacation week at Pittsfield; 1 September, he starts classes at the Albany Academy and joins the Ciceronian Debating Society; fall, Gansevoort's business runs into debt, and their mother mortgages most of her inherited property.

1837   March, Herman has to withdraw from the Albany Academy; April, Gansevoort's business fails in the year's financial panic; June, Herman goes to Pittsfield to run the farm when his uncle Thomas departs for Galena, Illinois; fall, Herman takes a winter term in a rural school near Pittsfield, and teaches there until early 1838.

1838   In order to live cheaply Maria Melville (the spelling she was now using) takes her family into what seemed like exile at Lansingburgh, across the river and a dozen miles north of Albany; November, Herman begins a course in surveying and engineering at the Lansingburgh Academy.

1839   March?, Melville completes his course but fails in his effort to gain employment on the Erie Canal; May, his first known fiction, "Fragments from a Writing Desk," appears in a Lansingburgh paper. Still jobless in June, he signs on a merchant ship for a voyage to Liverpool and back. In the winter, he teaches school at Greenbush, near Albany.

1840    Apparently unable to collect the meager pay promised him, Herman visits his uncle Thomas in Galena, on the Mississippi; at Christmas, still having found nothing to do, signs on a whaling ship, the *Acushnet*, at New Bedford, Massachusetts.

1841    Melville sails on the *Acushnet* from Fairhaven, Massachusetts, 3 January, for the Pacific; fall and winter, the *Acushnet* cruises through the Galápagos Islands.

1842    9 July, deserts with a companion at Nuku Hiva, in the Marquesas Islands, and flees inland, where he lives with the Typee tribe; 9 August, signs on an Australian whaler, the *Lucy Ann*; 24 September, crew members refuse duty in Tahiti, and, later joined by Melville, are laxly imprisoned by the British consul; November, Melville signs on a Nantucket whaler, the *Charles and Henry*, as a boatsteerer or harpooneer.

1843    In May, Melville is discharged at Lahaina, in the Hawaiian Islands; he works at Honolulu (as a pin-setter in a bowling alley and as a store clerk) then signs on the U.S. Navy frigate *United States* as an ordinary seaman; the ship cruises in the Pacific and the western coast of South America.

1844    October, Melville is discharged from the navy in Boston and visits his mother, four sisters, and youngest brother in Lansingburgh (now in slightly less precarious circumstances than when he left) and spends time in New York City with Gansevoort and their younger brother Allan, both now lawyers. Gansevoort is now famous as a great partisan orator, having just stumped the West for Polk. Melville writes out his adventures with the Typee tribe, from the point of view of an ordinary sailor who happened to possess, already, an extraordinarily appealing sensibility, and who had already tried out parts of his story as yarns at sea and ashore.

1845    Rewarded with the secretaryship of the American legation in London, Gansevoort carries the manuscript of *Typee* with him, and places it with the great publishing firm of John Murray.

1846    *Typee* appears first in England on 27 February as *Narrative of a Four Months' Residence among the Natives of a Valley of the Marquesas Islands; or, A Peep at Polynesian Life* then on 17 March in the United States (published by Wiley & Putnam) as *Typee: A Peep at Polynesian Life. During a Four Months'*

*Residence in a Valley of the Marquesas*, Melville's preferred title. The work is a sensation in both countries because of the freshness of the subject matter, hitherto described mainly by ministers intent on Christianizing the natives and by naval officers intent on recording information of economic and military importance. On 12 May Gansevoort dies in London, leaving Herman the oldest living son. In December Melville sells a new manuscript to Murray and to the Harpers (having sought a new publisher because John Wiley had forced him to expurgate the American edition of *Typee*).

1847    In February Melville tries in vain to find a government job in Washington, shortly before he publishes *Omoo*, which continues his adventures from his escape from Typee through his weeks in Tahiti and the neighboring Eimeo. In August he marries Elizabeth Shaw (Lizzie), the daughter of the Chief Justice of the Massachusetts Supreme Court (an old friend of Allan Melvill); the newlyweds set up housekeeping (with funds from Shaw) in a house in New York City large enough also to fit Melville's brother Allan and his new bride as well as Maria Melville and her four unmarried daughters. Melville becomes part of the literary circle of Evert A. Duyckinck and Cornelius Mathews.

1848    Melville extends his work on his third book, *Mardi*, a romantic and satirical allegory, far beyond the time he and his wife first think it is almost completed. Murray having rejected it as avowedly fictional, Melville finds a new British publisher, Richard Bentley.

1849    The Melvilles' first child, Malcolm, is born in February, and in spring the ambitious and over-literary *Mardi* is published, to mixed reviews and slow sales; as penance Melville writes at amazing speed *Redburn* (1849) and *White-Jacket* (1850); a friend says he wrote the latter book in only "a score of sittings." Goes to England to sell *White-Jacket* under new and threatening copyright rulings, and (abandoning plans for a twelve-month trip) makes a brief side-trip to Paris and the Rhine country before returning to London and home.

1850    Home in early February, Melville soon begins *Moby-Dick*. In July he takes his family to vacation in Pittsfield, and there meets Nathaniel Hawthorne and writes "Hawthorne and His Mosses." Soon afterwards he buys a farm near Pittsfield (which he names Arrowhead—now the home of the Berkshire County Historical Society), and establishes a routine for a winter of writing.

1851   In Pittsfield Melville goes into debt in order to make improvements on the farm (and perhaps in order to pay for plating his whaling book himself); works on the book during increasingly difficult circumstances; in October his second child, Stanwix, is born. In London *The Whale* is published in October 1851 to great acclaim even though by some accident it is published without the "Epilogue," and therefore seems to be a book by a first-person narrator in which that narrator perishes before writing the book. In America Melville substitutes a more memorable title at the last minute: *Moby-Dick*. The book is widely praised, but the free and easy tone toward religion (which had been largely censored out of the English edition) arouses much indignation, and many reviewers are cruel, imperceptive, and contemptuous (one calls the characters and Melville insane). Hawthorne praises *Moby-Dick* and offers to write a review of it as he leaves the Berkshires to return to eastern Massachusetts. In December Melville is angered by gossip in Pittsfield that the book is "more than Blasphemous."

1852   In January, distressed by the reviews of *Moby-Dick* and at its slow sales, then frustrated and angered when his publishers will give him for the manuscript of *Pierre* only twenty cents on the dollar (after costs) instead of fifty cents, Melville for a period of weeks does everything wrong that he can possibly do. He wrecks the finished or nearly finished short book, *Pierre*, by writing 150 more pages (about his hero—and himself—as an author) which he crudely interpolates into the manuscript. Then in May he destroys the continuity of his reception in England by refusing to let his publisher put the book out there in an expurgated form and with no advance: the British reviewers have no follow-up to *The Whale* (although one reviewer gets hold of one of the handful of copies of the American edition bound for sale in England). In May Melville defaults on the interest owed to T. D. Stewart for the loan made the previous year. When *Pierre* is published in New York late in July 1852 it provokes a firestorm of outrage, for it deals perturbingly with a series of false family relationships in one of which incest is openly hinted at. Everything Melville writes after *Pierre* is aftermath. Nothing he does can overcome the damage to his reputation in the United States; and the failure of *Pierre* to be published in England leaves his career truncated there, just at the time when a score or more of brilliant reviewers consider him one of the finest new writers in the English language. In November, and in each successive November and May for four more years he defaults on the payments due Stewart. From August till December he broods over a true story about a long-suffering Nantucket woman, and repeatedly urges Hawthorne to make fictional use of the material. In mid-December he decides to write the story himself.

1853　Melville spends several months writing the story he had tried to persuade Hawthorne to write. The week his daughter Elizabeth is born, in late May, he completes it, under the title *The Isle of the Cross*, but for some reason the Harpers do not publish it. In the late spring his failure to publish *The Isle of the Cross* is compounded by the failure of the family's efforts to secure him a post in a foreign consulate. Through the summer he writes short tales, and at the end of the year the first are published in *Putnam's Monthly* and *Harper's New Monthly*. In November Melville plans a new book on tortoise hunting and alludes to *The Isle of the Cross* as if it still exists.

1854　In July Melville begins serializing *Israel Potter* in *Putnam's*. Apparently he makes no further attempt to publish *The Isle of the Cross*, and perhaps destroys it.

1855　February, Melville is "helpless" from rheumatism; Frances, his fourth child, is born in March, the month Putnam's publishes the book form of *Israel Potter*. June, Melville suffers from sciatica. He does not complete the book on tortoise hunting.

1856　Dix & Edwards publishes *The Piazza Tales* in May. Stewart threatens to force the sale of the farm, and Melville must reveal his plight to his father-in-law. Shaw rescues him from financial disaster, as Melville puts up half the farm for sale. Concerned for Melville's health and sanity, Shaw through Melville's brother Allan arranges a prolonged tour for his son-in-law. After visiting Scotland, Melville goes to see Hawthorne in Liverpool, where his friend is consul, then sails to the Mediterranean.

1857    After a stopover in Egypt and a stay of three weeks in the Holy Land, Melville goes to Greece, Sicily, Naples, and Rome. *The Confidence-Man*, a satirical allegory on American optimism (completed before Melville left home) is published in London and New York on or around April Fools' Day (the date the action of the book occurs), earning him not a penny. Melville tours through northern Italy, Switzerland, Germany, and the Netherlands before returning to England and sailing for home in late May. In July Melville agrees to purchase a house in Brooklyn but changes his mind; in the fall he puts Arrowhead up for sale, but does not find a buyer. Beginning in November he lectures on "Statues in Rome."

1858    Lectures on "Statues in Rome" early in the year, then in the new season (December) on "The South Seas." Some reviewers are enthusiastic, but on most nights Melville makes a very bad impression (though in earlier years he had been called incomparable at dramatic storytelling).

1859    Lectures on "Traveling"—but he can book only three dates for the season.

1860    Melville gives his last lectures; in May, leaving a collection of poems for his wife and brother Allan to try to publish, he sails for Cape Horn and San Francisco in a ship commanded by his youngest brother, Thomas; he returns in November.

1861    Again proposed by his family for a consulship, Melville goes to Washington office-seeking, but returns when his father-in-law dies; the family winters in Boston then New York City.

1862    Recovering from a siege of rheumatism, Melville returns to Pittsfield, where he again puts the farm up for sale; in November, after moving to a rented house in the village of Pittsfield, he is badly injured when thrown from a wagon in a freak accident. (Until this time, he had been known as a daring, even reckless driver; the accident makes him excessively cautious.)

1863    In October Melville and his family leave Pittsfield permanently (except for short visits), living thereafter in New York.

1864    In April Melville gets a firsthand glimpse of the Civil War when he visits a cousin serving in the Army of the Potomac.

1866   The Harpers publish four of Melville's poems about the war
       in *Harper's* and in August publish *Battle-Pieces and Aspects
       of the War*. On 5 December Melville at last receives a govern-
       ment job, as an inspector of customs in New York.

1867   In the spring Elizabeth Melville is so miserable in her marriage
       that her minister suggests she visit her brothers in Boston then
       refuse to return; in early May her brothers reject the idea as
       illegal and unwise. On 11 September the oldest son Malcolm,
       shoots himself; Lizzie waits all day for him to get up, and
       when Melville returns from work he forces open the door and
       finds Malcolm dead in his bed.

1868   In November Melville is mentioned in Sophia Hawthorne's
       edition of *Passages from the American Note-Books of Nathan-
       iel Hawthorne*.

1870   In June Melville is intimately described in an abridged entry
       (without his permission) in *Passages from the English Note-
       Books of Nathaniel Hawthorne*; from being more famous than
       Hawthorne, Melville begins to be known to some younger
       readers as an acquaintance of Hawthorne's.

1870-75   During his years in the Custom House Melville continues to
          write poetry, most notably the eighteen-thousand-line *Clarel*,
          about a group of travelers (American, English, Continental,
          and Near Eastern) in the Holy Land. In it Melville invents
          conversations he cannot have with anyone alive—on topics
          such as the decline in religious fervor, the leveling of American
          values, the unresolved issues of the French Revolution, the
          near-impossibility of believing in Christianity in the new sec-
          ular world.

1876-77   After (and possibly even before) publishing *Clarel* in June
          1876 Melville works on a much less ambitious and private
          project, two interrelated poems, "A Symposium of Old Mas-
          ters at Delmonico's" and "A Morning in Naples," along with
          prose sketches introducing their fictional narrators; he gives
          the whole project the inclusive working title of "Parthenope"
          (the pieces are now generally referred to as the "Burgundy
          Club Sketches").

1882   Melville's first grandchild, Eleanor Melville Thomas, is born
       to his daughter Frances.

1885   Nine pages of Melville's "not very interesting epistles" to Hawthorne (the scornful comment of T. W. Higginson in the February *Atlantic Monthly*) are included (without his permission) in Julian Hawthorne's *Hawthorne and His Wife*; Lizzie gives Melville a copy of the book in June. In this year (?) Melville writes one of his many sea-pieces, a ballad, "Billy in the Darbies," about a sailor the night before his execution for mutiny (a crime of which he is guilty). On 31 December Melville resigns from the Custom House.

1886   From the time of his retirement, Melville's wife silently puts the substantial sum of twenty-five dollars in his pocket every month with the tacit understanding that he can spend it on books and prints without depleting the family larder. In February the Melvilles' second son, Stanwix, dies in San Francisco. After his retirement Melville works on the "Burgundy Club" material and at intervals he also works on a prose account of Billy Budd which began as a headnote to the ballad.

1888   Early in the year Melville makes a fair copy of *Billy Budd* but is led into further revisions. In September De Vinne publishes for Melville *John Marr and Other Sailors, with Some Sea-Pieces*. In November Melville turns again to the story of Billy Budd.

1890?   Melville drops the prose sketches from the "Burgundy Club" manuscripts; the poems he now entitles "At the Hostelry" and "Naples in the Time of Bomba."

1891   In April Melville again thinks he has finished *Billy Budd*, but is drawn into further revisions. In June Caxton Press publishes his *Timoleon and Other Ventures in Minor Verse*. On 28 September, with *Billy Budd* not quite completed, Melville dies.

# Bibliographical Note

References to *Billy Budd, Sailor* are to the edition of Harrison Hayford and Merton M. Sealts, Jr. (Chicago: University of Chicago Press, 1962). The context will make it clear whenever I refer to *Billy Budd, Foretopman* in one or another text prepared by Raymond Weaver or by F. Barron Freeman. Citations of Melville's works other than *Billy Budd* are to volumes in the Northwestern-Newberry Edition, published or forthcoming. I quote from *The Letters of Herman Melville*, ed. Merrell R. Davis and William H. Gilman (New Haven: Yale University Press, 1960). In 1983 the New York Public Library acquired papers of Melville's sister Augusta which had come to rest in a barn in upstate New York, and smaller but significant troves have also some to light since the publication of the standard documentary life of Melville, Jay Leyda's two-volume *The Melville Log* (New York: Harcourt, Brace, 1951) and since its republication with a supplement (New York: Gordian Press, 1969). In the "Chronology" and elsewhere in this volume events in Melville's life are sometimes assigned dates different from those in standard sources. In all such cases the evidence for my dating is in the forthcoming Gordian Press three-volume *The New Melville Log* by Jay Leyda and Hershel Parker.

Since criticism of *Billy Budd, Sailor* has so far evaded the implications of the Hayford-Sealts Genetic Text, there is little point listing individual essays or collections of essays, even a collection so sophisticated in matters of literary theory (though not textual theory) as the first issue of *Cardozo Studies in Law and Literature* (Spring 1989). Anyone who wants to survey the history of criticism

on *Billy Budd, Foretopman* and *Billy Budd, Sailor* will find all he
or she needs to know in a handful of guides. The first three and a
half decades of commentary are noted in Brian Higgins, *Herman
Melville: An Annotated Bibliography, 1846-1930* (Boston: G. K.
Hall, 1979) and Brian Higgins, *Herman Melville: A Reference
Guide, 1931-1960* (Boston: G. K. Hall, 1987); the publisher
changed the title, but the 1931-60 volume is in fact a continuation
of the previous one. Stanley T. Williams wrote the Melville chapter
in *Eight American Authors* (New York: Modern Language Associ-
ation, 1956) and one of his Melville students at Yale, Nathalia
Wright, wrote the Melville chapter in *Eight American Authors,
Revised Edition* (New York: W. W. Norton, 1971). Hayford and
Sealts included an extensive "Bibliography" (up to early 1962) in
their edition of *Billy Budd, Sailor*. For other 1962 items see the
*PMLA Annual Bibliography*. Beginning the next year, writing on
*Billy Budd* is discussed in the Melville chapter in each *American
Literary Scholarship: An Annual*, published by Duke University
Press. (The chapters have been written successively by Willard
Thorp, Merton M. Sealts, Jr., Hershel Parker, Robert Milder, and
Brian Higgins.) Of considerable historical interest is William T.
Stafford's *Melville's "Billy Budd" and the Critics* (Belmont, Cali-
fornia: Wadsworth, 1961), and his second edition for the same
publisher (1968). Also of historical interest are Haskell S. Sprin-
ger's *The Merrill Studies in "Billy Budd"* (Columbus, Ohio:
Charles E. Merrill, 1970) and Robert Milder's *Critical Essays on
Melville's "Billy Budd, Sailor"* (Boston: G. K. Hall, 1989).